Sewing Quilted
Patchwork
JACKETS

**Four Approaches,
Ten Distinctive Designs,
Two Downloadable Patterns**

Sewing Quilted Patchwork Jackets

Landauer Publishing, www.landauerpub.com, is an imprint of Fox Chapel Publishing Company, Inc.

Project Team
Managing Editor: Gretchen Bacon
Acquisitions Editor: Amelia Johanson
Editor: Christa Oestreich
Designer: Wendy Reynolds
Studio Photographer: Mike Mihalo
 Proofreader & Indexer: Jean Bissell

ISBN 978-1-63981-079-6

Library of Congress Control Number: 2024942285

To learn more about the other great books from Fox Chapel Publishing, or to find a retailer near you, call toll-free 800-457-9112, send mail to
 903 Square Street,
 Mount Joy, PA 17552,
 or visit us at www.FoxChapelPublishing.com.

We are always looking for talented authors. To submit an idea, please send a brief inquiry to acquisitions@foxchapelpublishing.com.

Note to Professional Copy Services:
The publisher grants you permission to make up to six copies of any quilt patterns in this book for any customer who purchased this book and states the copies are for personal use.

Printed in China
First printing

Sewing Quilted
Patchwork
JACKETS

**Four Approaches,
Ten Distinctive Designs,
Two Downloadable Patterns**

Rae Cumbie and Carrie Emerson

Landauer Publishing

Contents

For more jacket inspiration, view the Photo Gallery on our website.

42

52

60

82

90

126

Introduction

Inside this book, you will find 10 fabulous quilted coats and the multisize patterns to make each one successfully for sizes from kid to adult. The patterns include style options for a front band or shirt collar opening, multiple hem lengths, a hemmed or cuffed sleeve, and three methods for lining the jackets. So many choices to make the quilted jacket or coat of your dreams!

The defining feature of a quilted jacket or coat is the three layers of fabric that are quilted together to create a warm and comfortable garment.

- **The outer layer** is like the decorative quilt top. It can be as simple as a single fabric or a complex pieced design featuring multiple fabrics. Ultimately, it will be decorated with quilting threads.
- **The middle layer,** like the batting of a quilt, is hidden between the inner and outer layers. Your choice of loft material will determine the thickness, warmth, and suppleness of the finished jacket.
- **The inner layer,** which lies against the wearer's body, is like the quilt backing. It can be a simple lining fabric to protect and support the jacket, or it can be as finished as an outer layer to create a reversible jacket.

The quilted jacket sections are assembled in the same way for every project, so once you have practiced our construction method, you'll find those steps easy. The layers of each jacket section are stacked and quilted separately before assembling the jacket. Each option for adding the lining and finishing the jacket includes appropriate techniques for finishing the seams, hemming, and other details.

This book is written for both quilters and garment sewers, bringing together two worlds of craft that we love. Look for special tips to guide quilters who are new to garment sewing and garment sewers who are new to quilting. We encourage everyone to start with the simplest option, named "wholecloth" for both adults and kids, which will help you learn the steps of creating a quilted jacket. Then, build skills as you sew more complex projects, including patchwork and pieced jackets, coats that incorporate orphan quilt blocks, a repurposed quilt, or a fully reversible piece.

Included with this book are patterns for both the adult versions (size XS to 3XL) and the child versions (size 2 to 12) of every jacket. They are sized to fit well while offering enough ease of movement for a three-layer garment. The square armhole design is comfortable to wear, easy to construct, and especially well-suited for joining the quilted layers.

Creating a quilted jacket is a labor of love! It's an artistic process that should be savored, not rushed. That's why we have named our pattern the Opus Quilted Jacket and Coat—the finished garment is a masterpiece! We hope you will enjoy the process almost as much as the resulting garment. Let's get sewing!

—Rae and Carrie

These jackets can be customized in almost every way to match your style and size.

Plan the Opus Jacket or Coat

Here are tips for selecting materials and planning the design before you move onto making the jacket or coat. Construction of this garment can be formulaic, so the real variety starts at the very beginning by mixing and matching pieces, picking fabric, and adding your own flair. It's time to plan a quilted jacket that you'll be proud to wear or to give to a special adult or child in your life.

Design Guidelines

When designing a quilted jacket, we follow several essential guidelines. Follow these to help you select and plan the decorative outer layer for your quilted jackets and coats. Look at the project jackets in this book to see these principles at work.

Design Spaces

The most complex or extravagant designs or handiwork are best featured on the jacket's primary spaces. Consider the two fronts and the back as the primary design spaces, especially the highly visible shoulder area above the high horizontal balance line. It is also where the jacket needs the most support, which piecing and quilting provide naturally. The center back is another very visible primary space. Small details can be featured on the front band and collar.

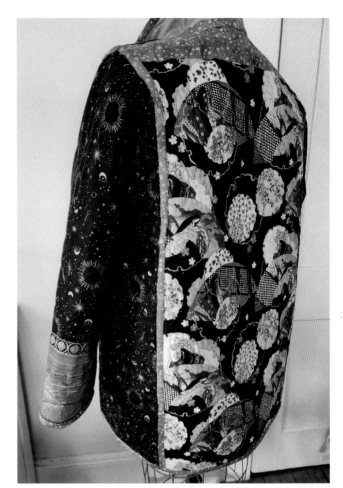

The front and back are best for showing off a design or print, while the sides and sleeves are typically less intricate.

Consider the sleeves and sides as secondary spaces, a complementary extension of the primary jacket spaces. Place the subtler prints or darker colors in the secondary spaces, and piece or quilt them less intensively. The softer the secondary spaces, the more naturally the jacket will hang.

Balance

When planning your decoration on the first layer, think of your jacket as an integrated whole that needs a balanced look overall. If you prefer symmetry, lay your designs out as mirror images, right to left. If you prefer a more asymmetrical design, sketch your ideas first to make sure the prominent design elements are balanced from right to left and front to back.

Symmetry looks beautiful on a coat, but you may end up preferring an asymmetrical design like this one.

Repetition

Repeating decorative elements in more than one place helps to achieve a well-integrated look, allowing the eye to move easily around the jacket. The repeated uses do not need to be exact reproductions, but simply carry each fabric or design element into at least three places on the jacket. For example, repeat the fabric on the cuffs, the side panels, and as an element in the back.

Color

Place closest to your face the colors that appeal to you or that complement you. Use the strongest and brightest colors of your palette in the primary design spaces while placing the darker colors and subtler prints in the areas you wish to downplay.

By employing lots of purple and yellow, opposite colors on the color wheel, this jacket becomes very bright and modern.

Choosing fabrics and a color palette for a project like this is very personal! Typically, we look for fabrics that complement one another when planning a mixed-fabric garment. If you are not confident about blending fabrics, selecting fabrics from within a designer fabric collection is a great way to ensure that your fabrics will blend harmoniously. Colors with high contrast, such as opposites on the color wheel, can also make a striking quilted jacket or coat.

Scale

The scale of the piecing and the designs on fabric are both important elements for your finished piece. Keep the scale in proportion to the size of the wearer and to the size of each pattern piece's section. For example, large quilt blocks can overwhelm a smaller person or child. A large design or panel can be accommodated

Tip

While planning a jacket or coat, test your ideas. Pin your fabrics to the mock-up, on a dress form, or onto a hanger to see your designs. Step back several feet or take a photo to get a better perspective on how the elements work together over the whole jacket.

A large image like this needed to go on the back. But the rest of the design was left fairly simple to allow the figure to shine.

in the back of the jacket or can be split into two pieces for the front, being mindful of design elements that may be lost.

With a large print, determine the part of the print you most want to be featured, and place it in a primary space that can accommodate the print. Small-scale designs can be accommodated in more places on the jacket, but their prominence may be diminished on a jacket when in motion. Make a mock-up and use it as your guide for the best size, proportion, and placement of design elements on your jacket.

Material Selection

You can create quilted jackets, coats, and vests from almost any type of fabric. Knowing when and where you will wear the jacket helps narrow your choices. Will you wear this garment in the spring and fall or winter? What are the typical temperatures in your area? Will this jacket or coat be worn for everyday work, play, a special occasion, or evening wear? Consider these

Quilt makers will be familiar with the three quilt layers, which is another way that this garment is approachable for all sewers.

factors when choosing materials for a quilted coat or jacket.

Choose high-quality fabric, batting, lining, thread, and closures to create a quilted jacket that will stand up to regular wear and last a lifetime.

Outer Layer

The decorative outer layer of the projects in this book are all created with stable cotton fabrics, most of them typical "quilting cottons" or similar weight that you can find at many fabric and quilt shops. Cotton is easy to work with, readily available, comes in an infinite array of colors and prints, and is an excellent choice for a pieced first layer.

When considering other fabrics for the outer layer, keep in mind the weight and bulk of the fabric once it is pieced and layered. Avoid fabrics with any stretch when piecing.

Middle Layer

The middle layer is part of what makes the quilting stitches stand out. The type of batting or other loft material you select affects how thick or thin and how supple or stiff your jacket

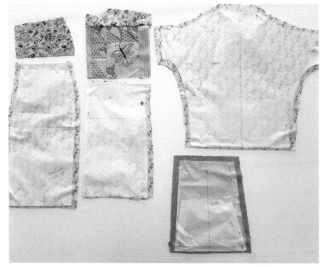

Patterns will be used to cut each layer, but the outer layer will typically use the most interesting fabric.

will be when finished. It also affects the warmth of the coat, so take your personal comfort into consideration as you choose your middle layer.

- Lighter, more supple battings enhance the three-dimensional look of quilting without making the jacket stiff or bulky. These battings often contain some portion of bamboo, rayon, or silk.

- Polyester battings add warmth to the coat but are less breathable.
- Cotton battings are widely available; we recommend choosing the thinner options for a more supple jacket.
- Wool battings are often mentioned as good for garments, but we find they frequently shrink and stiffen when pressed with a steam iron.
- For less-textured quilting or for less warmth and weight, choose fabric rather than batting for the middle layer, such as flannel, muslin, or cotton.

Look at the batting chosen for each project in this book to see how it affects the finished garment. Make some samples to test your selections.

Lining fabric typically won't be seen, but it makes the garment more comfortable to wear.

Inner Layer

There are many fabric options for the inner layer (lining): silky, crisp, light, heavy, warm, pieced, or plain to name a few. Each offers advantages and disadvantages. Your selection will affect the comfort, appearance, and durability of your jacket.

- Cotton linings are breathable and quite stable for quilting but will stick to the clothing you wear beneath the jacket.
- Silky linings, whether man-made, silk, or rayon, move smoothly over your clothing. This makes the outerwear easier to pull on and wear but can be slippery and more challenging to sew. Silk fabrics come in a wide variety of weights from light, such as "china silk" or habotai, to luxurious, such as charmeuse. Man-made silky fabrics are generally less breathable and therefore warmer.
- Flannel-backed acetate is especially good for lining cold weather coats but should be dry-cleaned.

Avoid fabrics with any degree of stretch for lining. Don't feel limited to solid colors! The lining fabric can be a print, stripe, check, or even be pieced for a very fun interior.

When making a reversible jacket, the inner layer becomes a second outer layer. Choose coordinating fabrics for the third layer that complement your first layer. The reverse side can be pieced or embellished in the same way as the first side, or completely differently. Just remember that, in a reversible jacket, all layers will be quilted simultaneously.

Tip

After gathering your fabric choices, make some sample "quilt sandwiches" with your outer fabric, batting, and lining options to test which combination you like best. Get in the habit of making samples to assess your fabrics and techniques before putting them into your beautiful garment.

Thread

Thread selection also plays an important role in the finished quilted jacket or coat. For construction of the jacket, standard polyester or polywrapped cotton in a neutral color are fine choices. For quilting, cotton and polyester threads are strong and durable and will stand up to laundering; rayon and silk threads are more lustrous but are more challenging.

The thread used for quilting the layers together will be visible on the outside of the jacket and, if you choose a quilted lining, on the inside or reverse side as well. There are infinite options for thread—lighter or heavier weights, single or blended color, shiny or matte surface—in infinite color choices. All these thread characteristics will affect the final appearance of your jacket, so make test samples with the quilt sandwiches you created when choosing fabrics to assess the threads' qualities and color. At the same time, try out the type of quilting stitches you are considering for each project.

Tools for Making Quilted Jackets

Making a quilted jacket requires some basic tools. Ideally, set up well-lit workstations for cutting, sewing, and pressing near each other. It's a lifesaver to arrange your workspace with an elevated table if possible, especially for patterning, laying out, and cutting fabric. We frequently use inexpensive bed lifts to raise the table to a more comfortable height for our backs.

In addition to our eyes and our hands, these tools are very helpful in creating successful jackets.

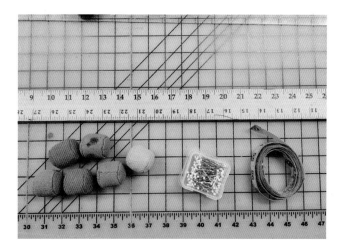

Working on Paper Patterns

The tools needed to trace the Opus pattern and make pattern adjustments include tissue or tracing paper, tape, a clear straight ruler with ⅛" markings, and pencils or pens in a few colors. We also find a curved design ruler useful when grading between sizes.

Anchoring and Pinning Fabric

We use a variety of pins suited to the need—glass-head dressmaker pins, pins with a tiny metal head for free motion quilting, and longer quilting pins to hold the layers together. The most important feature is that the pins be sharp! Clips may also be used if preferred, and weights for holding a pattern to the fabric for cutting.

Cutting Tools

We use several kinds of scissors in the process of creating a quilted jacket or coat. These include 8"–10" fabric shears for cutting out fabric, paper scissors, snips or embroidery scissors for cutting thread and working in small areas, and duck-bill scissors for grading seam allowances and trimming the batting out.

To cut fabric strips for piecing and bindings, we find a rotary cutter, ruler, and cutting mat to be more efficient and accurate than scissors.

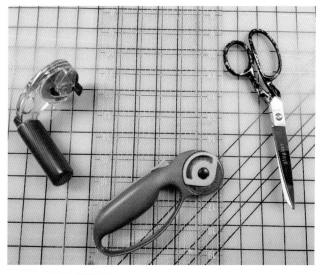

Marking Tools

There are several instances in which we advise marking on the fabric to guide your sewing. Choose marking tools with which the markings may be reliably removed from the fabric. We frequently use powdered chalk in a chalk roller. Fabric and quilt shops also market a variety of pencils, pens, or markers that will disappear with the application of heat or water. Be sure to test them on your scrap fabric first!

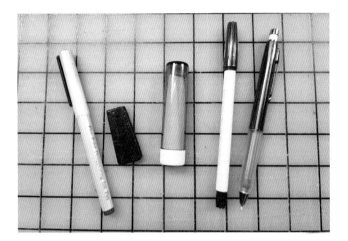

Pressing Tools

Your pressing station should have a full-size steam iron and an ironing board with one curved end. Felt mats and a small-size project iron may be helpful for small areas or for keeping in a location close to your sewing station. As garment sewers, we also regularly use a sleeve board for pressing the sleeve and cuff and a tailor's ham for pressing rounded seams, especially the dart and curved underarm of the Opus jacket.

Sewing Machine

A basic sewing machine with straight and zigzag stitches is sufficient for making a quilted jacket. For free motion quilting, you need to be able to drop the feed dogs on the machine. A serger for overlock stitching is helpful if you already have one, but zigzag and overlock stitches on a regular sewing machine can also perform the

Blind stitch foot

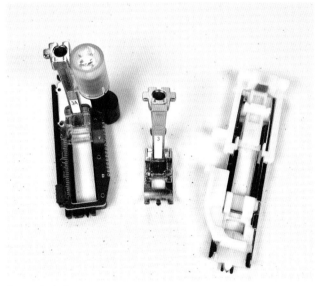

Buttonhole foot

needed function. Throughout the book, we point out specialty presser feet that will make the job easier if available. These include the

- walking foot, also known as an even-feed foot, to better manage straight stitching on multiple layers of fabric.
- seam guide bar to attach to a walking or other foot, to guide stitching in evenly spaced parallel lines.
- darning foot, stitch regulator, or other open-toed foot that permits you to see the stitching easily for free motion quilting.
- quarter-inch foot for piecing typical ¼" quilting seams.

Walking foot and seam guide bar

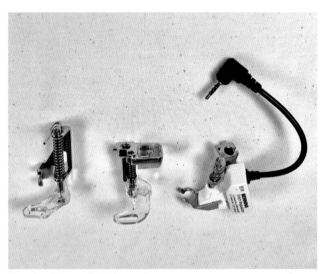

Darning foot and stitch regulator

- blind stitch or other foot with a metal guide for edge stitching.
- buttonhole foot for stitching multiple tidy buttonholes.

Needles

When sewing with a variety of threads, it's helpful to have multiple machine needles in different sizes on hand to find the best fit for your thread. We typically use universal and quilting needles for most stitching, but occasionally you might need a topstitching or denim needle for heavier threads or heavier fabrics. Also keep stitching needles in a variety of sizes on hand in your work area.

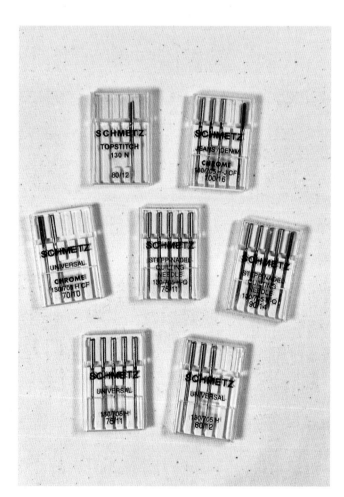

Make the Opus Jacket or Coat

Here, we lay out all the basic steps when it comes to making your jacket, whether that is designing a customized piece or following our instructions in the Projects chapter. You will likely be referring to this chapter constantly because it covers the important details throughout the rest of the book. For example, learn how to make and utilize the Opus pattern (page 27). We also recommend making a mock up and testing the fit for every project, which is described here. Finally, in-depth instructions for how to layer and quilt the fabric, make each style of jacket, and finish the piece are provided. So let's jump right in!

Choose the Project, Size, and Features

Before preparing pattern pieces or cutting fabric, you'll need to make some choices based on the coat or jacket you have in mind.

Kid Opus Size Chart				
	Body Measurements		Finished Measurements	
Size US	Chest	Hips	Chest	Hips
2	21"	22"	25½"	29"
4	23"	24"	27½"	31"
6	25"	26"	30"	33½"
8	27"	28"	32"	36"
10	28½"	30"	34"	38"
12	30"	32"	36½"	40½"

Adult Opus Size Chart				
	Body Measurements		Finished Measurements	
Size US	Chest	Hips	Chest	Hips
X-Small	30"–33"	33"–37"	38"	41"
Small	33"–36"	36"–40"	41"	44"
Medium	37"–40"	39"–43"	44"	47"
Large	41"–44"	42"–47"	49"	52"
X-Large	45"–49"	46"–52"	53"	57"
XX-Large	50"–54"	51"–57"	58"	62"
XXX-Large	55"–58"	55"–63"	61"	65"

See the Conversion Charts on page 183 for metrics.

Project. Go through the projects, starting on page 41. You can recreate the style exactly or customize it to your own taste. These projects were designed to use different techniques, so we recommend selecting one that has a good base to your idea; then you mix and match the styles as desired.

Pattern Size. Select the pattern size that will fit the wearer most closely based on the body and finished measurements in the Adult Size Table and the Kid Size Table on page 17 (see the Conversion Charts on page 183 for metrics). If the wearer's measurements correspond to different sizes in the upper and lower body, you can easily blend from one size to the other on this multisize pattern. These patterns are designed to have a relaxed fit with plenty of ease for wearing this coat or jacket over other clothing.

Front Style. Choose between the two jacket front styles based on the project directions. For projects featuring a front band, use the Band Front cutting lines on the pattern; follow the project directions to cut out the band pieces that will be attached after the jacket or coat is assembled. For projects featuring the shirt-style front overlap, choose the Shirt Front neckline and use the Collar pattern in the same size as the jacket neckline.

Sleeve Length. Select a sleeve length with or without a roll back cuff, as directed in your adult Opus project.

Opus Length. Select the desired length of your finished outerwear based on the project you are working on and personal preference. For the adult version, choose between the mid-hip length jacket and mid-thigh length coat; directions are included in Repurposed Quilt Duster (page 90) to extend the pattern for a mid-calf length duster with back vents. The child version is designed as a hip-length jacket.

It is a simple matter to adjust the length of either version to suit the wearer because of the square armhole construction and the relatively straight drop of the side seams. Make length adjustments at the hem cutting line, folding out paper to shorten and adding paper to lengthen. For the body of the jacket, the length adjustment must be made at the same place on the Front, Back, and Side patterns. Projects with a turned-up hem will be 1½" shorter than projects with a bound hem when finished, so factor that in when planning the cut length of the body of the coat or sleeves.

Details. Pockets are a fun addition to any jacket or coat, and there are different types of pockets shown in the projects. Piping can be a useful addition to a quilted jacket to repeat a fabric appearing elsewhere in the jacket, to draw attention to a particular feature, or to create a transition between two fabrics that don't match as closely as you might want. Because quilted jackets are already bulky, we prefer flat, or unfilled, piping for this decorative accent. This technique can be applied to insert piping on the front, between the sleeve/side and body of the jacket, or between a yoke and lower front or back. A yoke is another way to break up a design into smaller sections, which add detail and more ways to use your favorite fabric.

Closures. Snaps are an easy closure to apply and give you the option of changing to buttons and buttonholes later if you wish. Buttons add a fun and functional decorative element to the Opus collar style jacket. As you select buttons for your project consider: color, size (both scale relative to the garment and the size of buttonhole required), the number of buttons desired, and spacing to achieve closure.

Make the Pattern

The adult and kid patterns are very large, so we had to split them across multiple pieces of paper (tiled). You will need to reassemble them once printed out. This can be done by photocopying the patterns on pages 136 or downloading the files, through the QR code or the website: https://foxpatterns .com/sewing-quilted-patchwork-jackets/.

Scan for downloadable patterns

Customizing the PDF

Each PDF offers the option to hide any of the sizes that you don't want printed. Each size has its own layer, and we recommend turning off any extra layers that you don't need. This will remove extra lines that can cause confusion or potential mistakes.

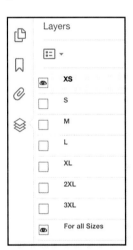

Go to the side panel on the left and click on the "Layers" option. Then turn layers on and off by clicking the eye next to each one. Be sure to *always* keep the "For all Sizes" and "pages" layers visible. Once you have adjusted the layers, you are ready to print.

Printing

The pattern has been broken up into pieces to be printed or photocopied at home on either Letter (8½" x 11") or A4 paper at 100%. The adult Opus pattern is 30 pages total, and the kids' version is 15 pages total. The page numbers are watermarked on each section for assembly. Make sure the option for "actual size" is selected.

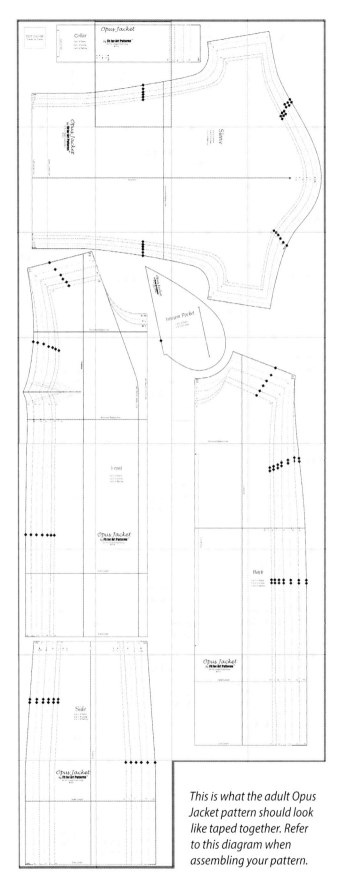

This is what the adult Opus Jacket pattern should look like taped together. Refer to this diagram when assembling your pattern.

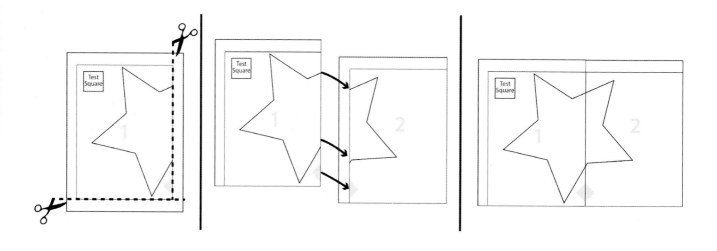

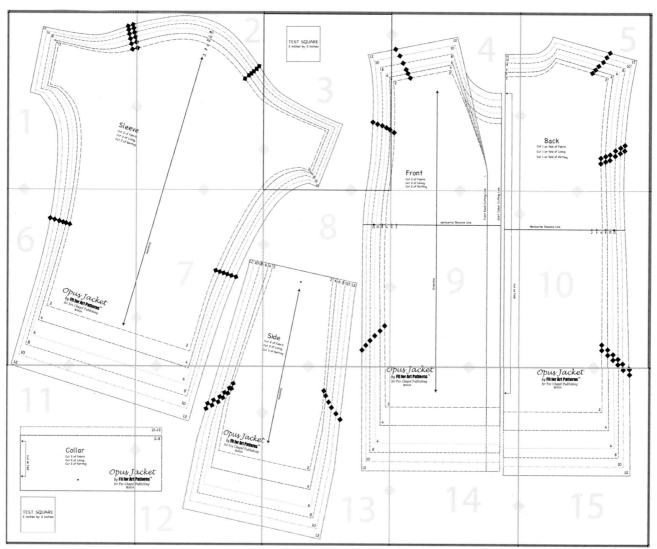

This is what the kid Opus Jacket patterns should look like taped together. Refer to this diagram when assembling your pattern.

Print or photocopy just the first page. Measure the test square to make sure that it accurately reflects the measurement listed. Then print the rest of the pages.

To assemble your tiled pattern (see the opposite page), cut off the right and bottom edges of each tiled page. Lay the pages out in numerical order, as illustrated on pages 19 and 20. Overlap page 1 on top of page 2 so that the right edge of page 1 lines up with the left side of page 2. Use the pattern lines and the gray diamonds as reference points; if there isn't a gray diamond, that side doesn't need to be taped to another page. Tape in place.

Repeat this process for the rest of the tiles, first working across each row on its own, and then connecting the rows. When complete, the adult Opus Jacket measures 74" long and the kids' Opus Jacket measures 36" long. Follow these directions carefully and be precise in your pattern assembly. Taking the time to line things up correctly now can help you avoid issues later in the project.

Trace the Pattern Pieces

It is much easier to lay out and cut the three fabric layers of a quilted jacket with a tissue pattern. If you are working with a pattern printed on copy paper, we advise tracing the pattern pieces for your project onto a more flexible material, such as tissue or Swedish paper. Be sure to trace all markings onto your tissue patterns, including grain lines, horizontal balance lines, notches, darts, and dots.

In typical garment sewing, the fabric is folded in half so that two Fronts, Sleeves, and Sides can be cut out simultaneously and the Back pattern cut on the fold. This method will work fine for cutting out the middle batting and inner lining layers. For pieced and quilted garments, however,

Tip

To avoid confusion, take a few minutes to label all your tissue pattern pieces on the marked side with the appropriate name to indicate right or left. For example, you will have a Right Front and a Left Front, and so on. It is also a great idea to note the size, date, and any fit adjustments onto the paper patterns for future reference.

it is very helpful to be able to see how all the sections will work together, especially at joining seams, before cutting. Having a full pattern makes this an easier task. By a "full pattern," we mean a pattern piece for every section: the Right and Left Fronts, Right and Left Sleeves, Right and Left Sides, and a full Back pattern.

To create a full Opus pattern, cut out a second copy of the Front, Sleeve, and Side patterns; turn them over; and transfer all markings onto the reverse side of the tissue. Trace the Back pattern onto a folded tissue, laying the center back along the fold. Cut the Back tissue out and open it to see a full Back with left and right sides. Transfer all markings to both sides of the full Back pattern. Do the same to make a full Collar pattern if needed.

Make a Mock-Up

Before you invest the time into making a quilted jacket, mock up your pattern to practice the construction steps. These jacket patterns feature square armhole construction, which is a bit different than set-in sleeve construction. You will feel more comfortable with the order of construction if you try it out in a mock-up.

The mock-up also ensures a satisfactory fit. Testing the fit is recommended before investing your time and materials into making any quilted jacket, especially for adult women

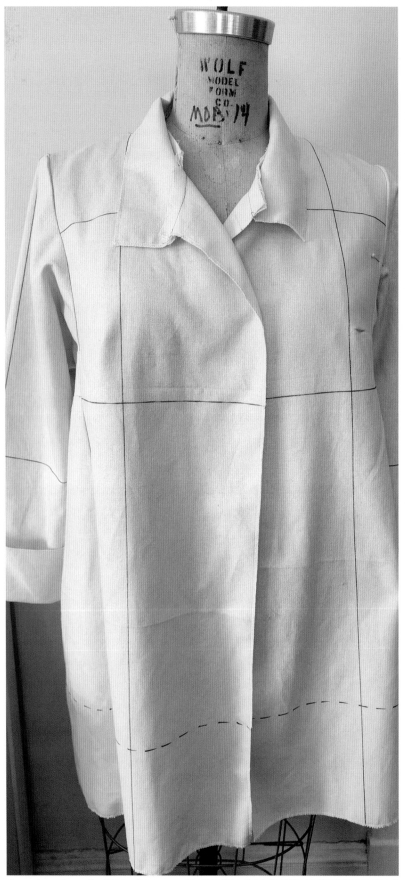

A mock-up is a valuable tool to assess the fit of the Opus jacket, make adjustments for personal fit, and plan the design.

whose curvy figures often require some fitting finesse. The mock up also comes in handy later when planning Opus projects or making length adjustments.

Follow these steps to make an Opus mock-up:

1. Cut out or trace the Opus pattern in the desired style and chosen size.

2. Choose a nonstretch bottom weight fabric, such as lightweight denim, cotton canvas, or similar fabric, in a light color so the fitting lines will be easy to see.

3. Cut the Back, Fronts, Sides, and Sleeves out of the mock-up fabric as directed. Cut around the notches so they will be easy to identify during construction and fitting adjustments.

4. Mark the end points of each grainline, horizontal balance line, and length line on the right side of each fabric section with a dark-colored permanent marker before removing the patterns. Mark darts and dots too.

Tip

Read our blog post for a detailed look at constructing a similar jacket with the same square armhole style.

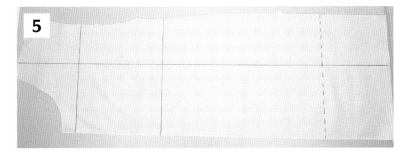

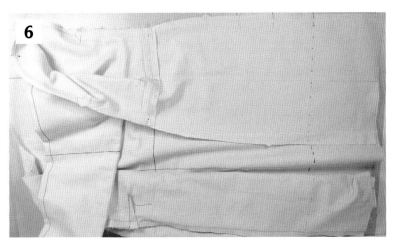

5. On each section's right side, use a straight ruler to connect the end points of the grainlines and horizontal balance lines (HBLs) with a dark permanent marker. The lines will form a fitting grid that must be easily visible.

6. Follow steps 1–5 of Construct the Opus Jacket or Coat (page 27) to make the mock-up. Use a machine basting stitch. Press the seam allowances as indicated at each step. Do not leave off the sleeves; they must be as comfortable and well-fitting as the body.

7. Test fit the Opus mock-up over clothing (step 6 of Construct the Opus Jacket or Coat). Look carefully at the grainlines and HBLs that should be, respectively, perpendicular and parallel to the floor in a perfectly fitting coat. The final mock-up should hang effortlessly from the shoulders to the hem with plenty of room for clothing layers under the body and sleeves of the coat.

8. Use the mock-up to assess the length of the coat or jacket and sleeves. Pin the mock-up to find your preferred length and make notes on your pattern or pattern adjustments. The Opus pattern length can easily be adjusted at the horizontal balance lines or the cutting lines, so long as the changes are made consistently to all affected pattern pieces.

7

Assemble the Layers

In this section, we walk you through the first stages of making an Opus quilted jacket or coat, from preparing the layers to quilting. Generally, the outer layer will be pieced separately; once complete, it can be layered with the batting and lining like any other fabric. Once you learn the technique, this process is easy!

Cut Out the Layers

The process of creating a quilted jacket or coat begins with choosing a project. Within each project, follow the instructions for creating the outer layer of the Opus—two Fronts, full Back, two Sides, two Sleeves, and front Band or Collar—which are unique to the project. In the reversible projects, there are specific instructions for creating the inner layer as well.

Each project includes recommendations for appropriate batting and lining choices. The batting and lining can be cut out with the standard set of tissue patterns on folded fabric. The diagram shows our recommended layouts for cutting 45" wide lining and batting; choose the appropriate layout based on the jacket size.

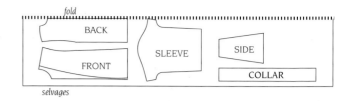

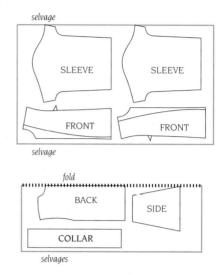

Pattern Layout Diagram

Be sure to cut all lining pieces with the pattern's grainline parallel to the selvage or fold of the fabric.

The process of quilting can cause some shrinkage, so we instruct you to cut out all layers of each pattern piece with an extra ½" on all perimeter sides. The excess will be trimmed

Establish Good Sewing Habits

- Set up well-lit workstations nearby one another for cutting, sewing, and pressing.

- Use sharp cutting tools, either scissors or a rotary cutter and mat.

- Sew consistent seams! These patterns include a ⅝" seam allowance on all pattern pieces. Sew a line of straight stitches on your sewing machine to test and measure the seam. If your machine markings do not give an accurate ⅝" seam, set up a seam guide on your machine for stitching straight even seams at the desired width. Use either a seam guide gadget or lay a strip of blue painters' tape on the machine bed to guide stitching consistently at ⅝" from the needle position.

- Press thoroughly as you go with a hot steam iron; the project directions indicate when pressing is required and whether to press the seam allowances open or to one side.

- For free motion quilting, set up sewing machine with decorative quilting thread in bobbin and spool, a new quilting or universal needle in an appropriate size for the thread, and an appropriate foot. It could be an open quilting foot, darning foot, or stitch regulator. Remember to drop the feed dogs for free motion quilting, allowing your hands to move the fabric in any direction.

away after quilting each jacket section. There is one exception to the extra ½" rule—the free-hanging lining for the Wholecloth Jacket, Jelly Roll and Appliqué Coat, and Wholecloth and Collage Jacket should be cut exactly to the pattern size, as this lining will not be quilted.

Prepare to Quilt

Prepare to quilt by connecting the layers of each section you are quilting, either the outer layer and batting or all three layers for a quilted-in lining. A reversible jacket needs all three layers to be quilted together. If only quilting two layers, a free-hanging lining won't be added to the jacket until step 8 of Construct the Opus Jacket or Coat.

Stack the layers of the fabric sandwich with the inner layer wrong side up, batting layer next, and finally the outer layer right side up. Secure the layers together so that they will stay in place while you quilt. Secure the layers by

- pinning them together at strategic places;
- bonding them together with a lightweight spray adhesive that will wash out; or
- hand basting them together at strategic points, if their alignment is critical. This might be important if you are trying to align designs on each side of a reversible jacket or are using a fabric with a lot of give.

In many instances, the project will direct you to trim away the batting within the seam allowances during the construction process to reduce bulk in the finished jacket. To make this easier, before you begin, mark the seam lines with chalk, disappearing marker or pencil, or basting thread on top of each quilting sandwich; do not quilt beyond those lines. Because the seam allowance is ⅝" and you have added ½" of additional fabric to allow for shrinkage, leave a 1" unquilted edge around each section. For

projects in which binding finishes the edges, you will not be trimming the batting, so quilt all the way to the raw edges that will be bound.

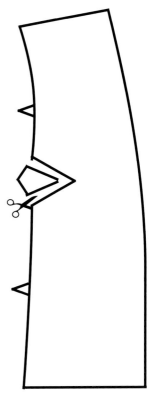

Dart Cutting Diagram

Using an iron, steam press the layers of each section separately, and then together to release any air that is between the layers.

For the adult Opus, pause before quilting the pattern sections that contain a dart (on the two Fronts and, if a rounded back adjustment has been made, at the Back neck). Lay the tissue pattern on each section and make sure the dart markings are aligned on all three layers. Adjust if needed. Cut away the batting, and only the batting, between the dart legs (see diagram above). This minimizes bulk when the dart is stitched later, during construction.

Quilt the Jacket Sections

Quilting techniques that work well for jackets, whether working by hand or machine, include stitch-in-the-ditch, echo stitching, stenciled patterns, channel stitching, stippling, free motion, motif stitching, kantha, and sashiko. You can use different quilting techniques on different sections of the jacket. The more you quilt, the more compact the sections will become, so limit the denser quilting to the primary spaces and use lighter quilting on the

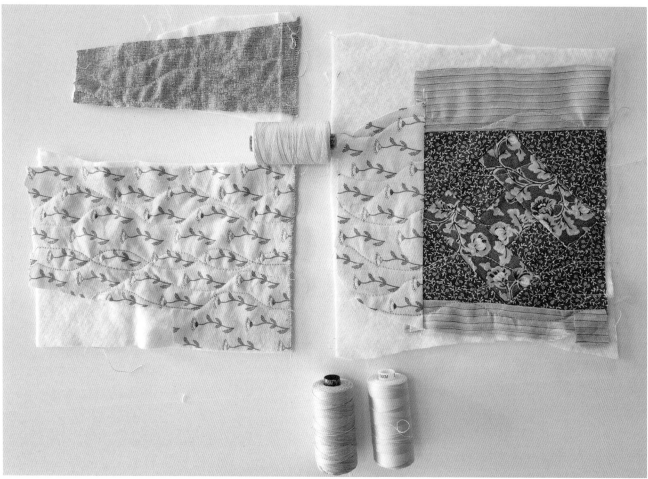

Test your thread and quilting design on a sample before working on your garment.

secondary spaces. Quilting at the lighter end of the spectrum results in more supple and successful jackets.

Each project includes a recommended quilting style that complements the piecing of the outer layer, but you may quilt each jacket section with a technique of your choice. It is essential to test possible quilting designs on sample quilt sandwiches. Make samples to test thread choices, needles, machine settings, and your technique. As you begin quilting the jacket sections, consider starting with the Side sections where your stitches will not be as noticeable.

When all the quilting is complete, press each jacket section again. Lay each section on the cutting table and re-pin the corresponding pattern piece to it. Sections with designs that need to match, such as the two Fronts, should be aligned on the table simultaneously. Trim away what remains of the extra ½" you added, snipping around the notches. Transfer markings for dots and darts to the prepared quilt section.

	wrong side		right side		**binding**		lining		facing

Illustration Legend (pages 27–34)

Construct the Opus Jacket or Coat

You are ready to assemble the sections into a jacket! The body of each quilted jacket or coat is constructed in the same order following these illustrated step-by-step directions. In most projects, you will be referred to this chapter to follow the Opus Construction directions, so it will be helpful to read through it before you start making jackets.

There are two different jacket styles outlined in these construction directions. Steps 1–6 are applicable to both styles. Steps 7–9 are the steps for completing the front band style, which is finished with turned-up hems and a front Band. Steps 10–13 are the steps for completing the shirt collar style, which is finished with a Collar, roll back cuff, and bound edges. It is difficult to add a free-hanging lining to the shirt collar style of jacket, so we have only included these directions for the front band style.

Please take note:

- For both the adult and child versions, a ⅝" seam allowance is included in the pattern. Make sure you are sewing a consistent ⅝" seam before assembling the jacket pieces.
- The illustrations show a dart on the fronts; if you are making the child's version, there will be no dart, and you will skip step 1.
- The illustrations are based on a jacket-length Opus. If you are making the coat or duster, your proportions will be somewhat different.

Opus Construction

Step 1—Stitch the Darts

Pin the dart on the wrong side of each adult Front by folding right sides together, matching the stitching lines. Sew from the seam line

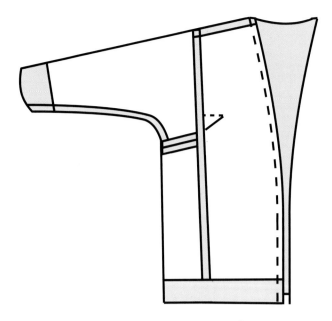

toward the point of the bust. Tie off the dart points rather than backstitching. Press the darts toward the hem.

Step 2—Sew the Shoulder Seams

Pin the Fronts and Back together at the shoulder, right sides together, matching notches. Sew each shoulder seam at ⅝", backstitching at the beginning and end. Trim the batting from the seam allowances, leaving about ⅛", then press the seam open. Finish the shoulder seams as directed in the project.

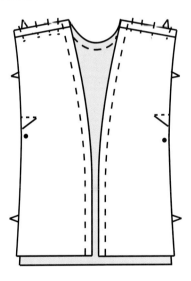

Step 3—Sew the Sleeves

OPTIONAL: Place gathering stitches along the upper edge of each Sleeve head. Set the sewing machine to the longest stitch length, and sew

gathering stitches

matching the dot on the Side to the Sleeve's underarm seam. Make sure that the single notch of the Sleeve and Side panel are both along one side of the Sleeve/Side unit and that the double notches are both along the other side. Sew the Sleeve to the Side panel with a ⅝" seam, backstitching at the beginning and end.

Trim batting from the seam allowances. Press seam allowances open or press both down toward the Side panel, finishing as directed in the project. Repeat for second Sleeve and Side.

two rows of gathering stitches along the curved upper edge of each Sleeve between the notches, one row at ¼" and the second row at ½" from the edge of the fabric. Leave thread tails of at least 2" at the beginning and end of each row and do not backstitch. Remember to change the stitch length back to standard stitch length when finished sewing gathering stitches.

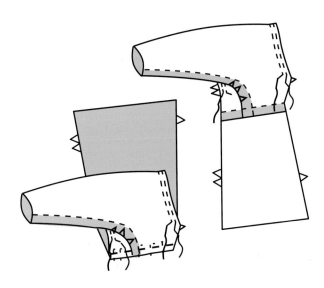

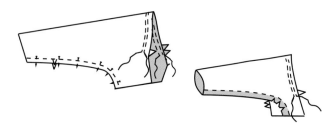

Fold a Sleeve in half, right sides together, matching notches along the underarm seam, and pin. Sew a ⅝" seam, backstitching at the beginning and the end. Trim batting from the seam allowances. Clip underarm curve with ⅜" deep snips. Press seam allowances open or toward the back, finishing as directed in the project. Repeat for the second Sleeve.

Step 4—Attach the Sleeves to the Sides

Open out the bottom of one Sleeve. Pin it right sides together to the top edge of one Side,

Step 5—Insert the Sleeve/Side Unit

Lay the body of the jacket on the table right side up. Turn the Sleeve/Side units right side out.

Lay the back of one Sleeve/Side unit on top of the jacket Back, right sides together, matching the double notches and matching the Sleeve/Side seam to the dot on the jacket Back. Pin the back of the Sleeve/Side to the jacket Back from the armhole notch to the hem.

Pull the jacket Front down over the front of the Sleeve/Side, matching the single notches and matching the Sleeve/Side seam to the dot on the jacket Front. Pin the Sleeve/Side front to the jacket Front from the armhole notch to the hem.

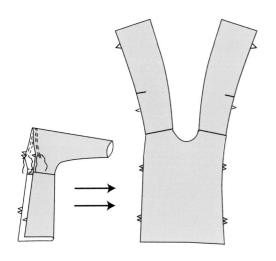

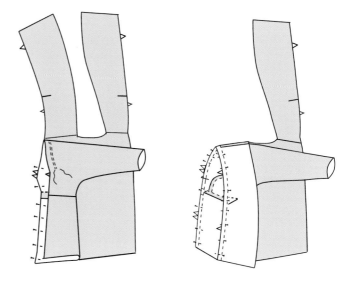

Once the Sleeve/Side is pinned in place, pin the dot at the top of the sleeve to the shoulder seam; ease the Sleeve into the shoulder of the jacket, pinning along the ⅝" seam line. If using, pull the optional gathering threads gently on the wrong side of the Sleeve to assist with easing the Sleeve head into the armhole. Reposition and add pins if needed to keep the sections aligned as you sew.

Place the pinned jacket under the sewing machine presser foot with the Sleeve/Side unit facing up and the Front/Back against the feed dogs. Carefully stitch a ⅝" seam from one hem, over the shoulder, and to the other hem. Backstitch at the beginning and end of the seam.

Stop every few inches and rearrange the jacket fabric so it is not bunching up underneath. At the shoulder seam, drop the needle, raise the presser foot, and shift the fabric. Then lower the presser foot to slowly stitch down the second Side to the hem edge.

Remove the jacket from the sewing machine and check the seam on both the outer and inner layer for smooth stitching. If there are places where the fabric has been caught incorrectly, remove the stitching in and around the caught fabric. Restitch the seam smoothly. Once

satisfied, press the seam allowances together away from the jacket and toward the Sleeve/Side. Do not trim batting from the seam allowances until you have tested and adjusted the fit in step 6.

Repeat these step 5 instructions to insert the second Sleeve/Side unit into the body of the jacket.

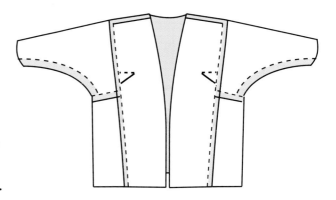

Test the Fit and Adjust

Step 6—Test the Fit

Try the jacket on right side out. The Opus Jacket or Coat is designed to have a relaxed fit so it can be worn over clothing. When trying on the jacket at the fitting stage, wear clothing underneath to accurately check the fit. Close the

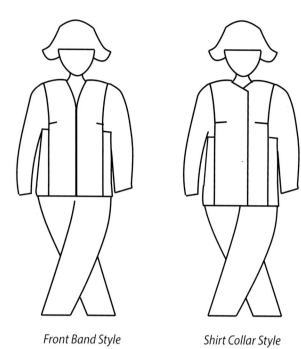

Front Band Style   Shirt Collar Style

jacket as directed in the pattern directions. In the front band style, the unfinished jacket fronts should just meet in the center of your body. In the shirt collar style, the unfinished jacket fronts should overlap by 2".

There should be enough ease through the body and shoulders that the coat sits closely but not tightly on the body. You may want to make fitting adjustments to your jacket at this stage because the quilted garment often hangs differently from the mock-up. Garment ease is a very personal choice, so make changes to increase or release the side seams to achieve a fit that is comfortable for you.

Try the coat on again to test the change before continuing to the construction process. Note any changes made on the paper pattern, so the fit will be improved the next time you use the Opus pattern.

When satisfied with the jacket's fit, trim the batting out of the seam allowances along the Side seams. Press seam allowances toward the Sleeve/Side unit, finishing seams as directed in your project.

Front Band Style

If constructing a project with a collar, skip ahead to the directions in steps 10–13 (page 32).

Step 7—Hem the Jacket and Sleeves

Try the jacket on again to determine the finished length you prefer. While the pattern has a 1½" hem allowance, you can choose your length during this test fit. Mark the hem of the body and sleeves to your desired length with pins or a removable-marking method. Trim away fabric that extends beyond the additional 1½" needed to turn up the hem in the sleeves and body of the jacket. If desired, machine stitch along the raw edge with a straight, zigzag, or overlock stitch to prevent fraying.

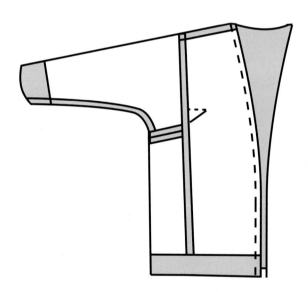

Press the hem up along the line you have marked on the sleeves and body of the jacket. Stitch the hems in place by hand, burying the thread between the layers of the jacket.

Step 8—Free-Hanging Lining

Skip ahead to step 9 if your project has a quilted-in lining or is reversible.

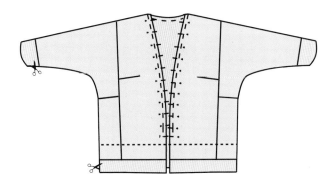

Cut all pattern pieces from the lining fabric. Follow Opus Construction steps 1–5 to assemble the lining, including any fit adjustments made in step 6.

Lay the quilted jacket right side out on a table, and place the assembled lining inside the jacket, wrong sides together. Beginning at the center of the back, pin the lining to the jacket body along the neck edges, matching shoulder seams and any other marks you have made as you move down each Front toward the hem. When you get

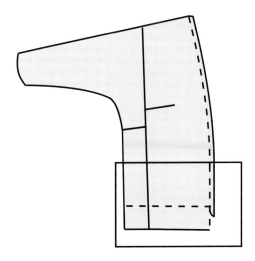

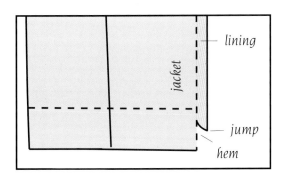

to the hem, the lining will appear too long. The extra length will be used to create a small pleat, known as a jump, to allow your jacket to move easily at the hem.

Stitch with a basting stitch all around the jacket front, ⅜" in from the raw edge, to secure the lining and jacket layers together. Stop basting 3"–4" from the hem on each side of the jacket Front.

Trim the lining to ½" longer than the hemmed jacket and Sleeves. Press the lining under by ¼"–½". Pin the pressed edge of the lining to the jacket and Sleeve hems, just covering the "raw" edge of the finished hem. Hand stitch the lining to the hem finishes.

Press the lining so that the jump lies flat against the hem. Finish basting the lining to the jacket along the center-front edge.

To make sure it hangs in a balanced way and that the lining does not hang below the hems, put the jacket on a hanger or dress form or try on the jacket. Correct if necessary.

Step 9—Prepare and Apply the Band

Measure jacket from the center Back to the hem and add 2". Cut two Bands with these dimensions: the length you have calculated x the width directed in your project. Add supports or batting to the Band pieces as directed in the project.

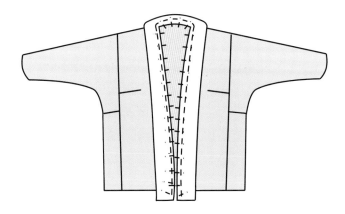

Sew the two Band pieces together along one short side. Trim the batting from the seam allowances and press the seam open.

Fold the Band in half lengthwise, wrong sides together, and press. Open the Band to its full width. Pin one side of the Band to the jacket edge, right sides together, starting at the center back and working out toward the hems. Ease the Band to the neck edge around the curves, pinning along the ⅝" seam line. Sew in place. Clip the seam allowances around the neck curve and shoulder area.

Trim the batting from the seam allowances. Press the seam toward the band and away from the jacket body. Press the long, unsewn edge of the Band under by ⅝".

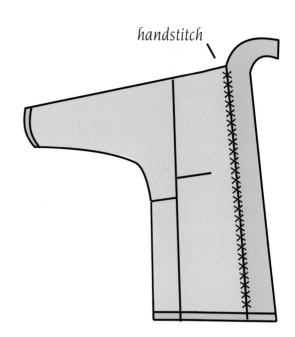

handstitch

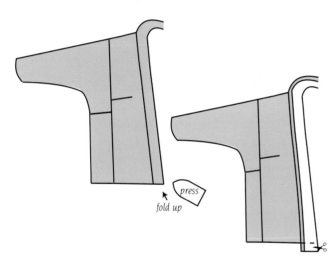

press
fold up

Turn ends of Band up to the jacket length and press. Open out the pressed Band length; reverse the folded ends of Band right sides together, and stitch just below the pressed fold from the outer edge to seam allowance. Turn the Band back to the right side to make sure the bottom of the Band lines up with the jacket hem. If the jacket and Band hems are not the same length, correct the placement of the stitch line. Turn the Band wrong side out and trim off the excess fabric below the seam, leaving about ¼"; clip the corner to reduce bulk.

Pin the pressed edge of the Band to the inside of the jacket, covering the seam line. Hand stitch the Band in place.

Follow the directions in your project to finish the Band and to add closures.

Shirt Collar Style

Step 10—Prepare and Insert the Collar

Cut out two Collars from the fabric and one Collar from the batting in your size. Prepare and quilt the Collar as directed in your project.

Lay the quilted Collar on the jacket with the side you want against your neck facing up and the other side against the jacket. Ease and pin

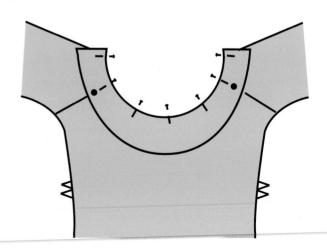

the Collar into place, matching the center back of the Collar to the center back of jacket (fold lines) and matching the dots on the Collar to the shoulder seams. The short edges of the Collar should line up with the front edges of the jacket. Because collars and necks have different curves, easing is required to connect them at the ⅝" seam line and to allow them to lie smoothly when completed. Baste the Collar to the jacket by hand or machine.

Check the seam on both sides for smooth stitching. If there are places where the fabric has been caught incorrectly, remove the stitching that is in and around the caught fabric, and restitch the seam smoothly. Once satisfied, restitch the entire collar seam with standard-length stitches.

Trim batting from the seam allowances, clip the neckline curves, and grade the seams.

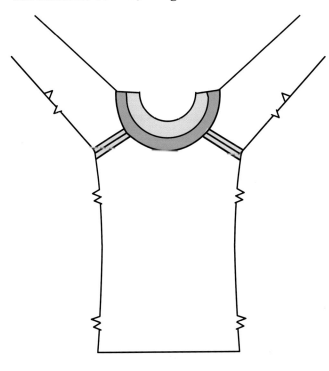

Cover the collar seam with binding as directed in your project, using the Reversible Seam Binding technique (page 37).

Step 11—Prepare the Hems and Roll Back Cuff

Try the jacket on to determine the finished length you prefer. Mark the hem of the body and sleeves to your desired length with pins or a removable-marking method. For the body of the jacket, trim away the fabric that extends beyond the desired hem length.

The roll back cuff should turn up at least 2". While trying on the jacket to assess the length, roll back the cuff so the quilted-in lining is visible. Unroll the cuff and trim away any excess that is not needed for the cuff.

Step 12—Finish the Edges with Binding

Follow this order to successfully bind the coat edges. Follow the directions in your project to choose the width of the binding. Each step is finished with the Classic Binding Technique (page 38). *Finish each step with a hand or machine finish before moving on to the next binding step.*

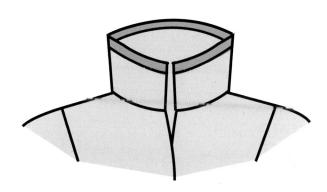

a. Measure the long, unfinished collar edge and prepare binding for this length. Follow the Classic Binding Technique to finish the top edge of the collar.

b. Measure the Center Fronts of the jacket, add 1", and prepare two pieces of binding at this length. Pin the binding to the Center Fronts with the extra 1" extending beyond the collar

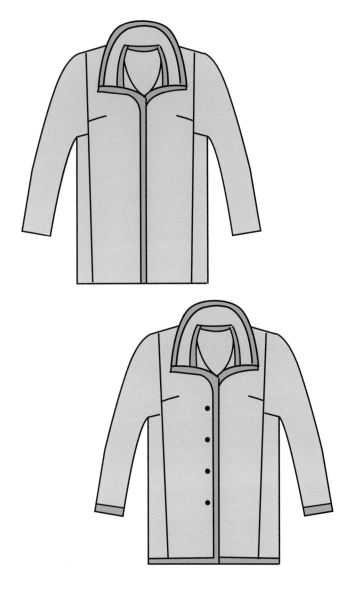

Step 13—Add Closures

Follow the directions in your project to choose and create the desired closures. Because there is a 2" overlap, buttons up to 1½" in diameter may be used to secure the front.

Finishing Techniques

Throughout this book, several different techniques are used to finish the seam allowances inside a coat or jacket in which the seams will not be covered with a free-hanging lining. These techniques protect the exposed seams from wear and tear and provide an attractive finish to the garment with minimal bulk. You will want to refer to this chapter for many of the projects. While we prompt you to utilize a particular seam-allowance finish for each project, you may choose to use an alternate technique when appropriate for the materials and situation.

The outer edges of the shirt collar style Opus Coat or Jacket are finished and protected with binding in lieu of a traditional facing to reduce bulk. Half of the projects in this book are finished with the Classic Binding technique at some or all edges and finished with the Reversible Binding technique where the collar is joined to the jacket. The reversible jackets also incorporate the Reversible Seam Binding technique to cover all additional seams.

Most of the bindings included in the book are bias bindings, although there are many straight edges where straight-of-grain bindings will also work. For example, several bindings in the Reversible Vest feature straight-of-grain bindings to take advantage of a directional print. To accommodate the bulk at the edges and seams of quilted coats, choose a binding with at least a ½" finished width. Refer to the project instructions for additional information about suggested binding width.

to finish that edge. Follow the Classic Binding Technique to finish the Center Fronts.

c. Measure the circumference of the hem edge and add 2". Prepare the binding for this length. Pin the binding to the hem with an extra 1" extending beyond each end. Follow the Classic Binding Technique to finish the hem.

d. Measure the circumference of the sleeve edge and add 1". Prepare two pieces of binding for this length. Use a ½" seam to sew each binding piece into a circle and press the seam allowances open. Pin one edge of a binding to each sleeve edge, matching the binding seam to the sleeve seam. Follow the Classic Binding Technique to finish the sleeves.

Seam Finishing Techniques

Machine Stitching

The simplest and quickest method for finishing seam allowances is to contain the edges with machine stitching. These machine finishes will prevent the fabric in the seam from unraveling and will provide a neat appearance. Take the time to test the stitches and to determine the optimal stitch width and length on your quilted test scraps before moving to the jacket's seam allowances.

For these quilted projects, the finishing stitches should not be done until after the seam is sewn and the batting removed from the seam allowances. If the seam allowance is pressed open, each side of the seam allowance must be finished separately. If the seam allowance is pressed to one side, both seam allowances can be finished together.

- **Zigzag:** Virtually all modern sewing machines can be used to zigzag along the raw edge of a seam allowance. Set your sewing machine to a zigzag stitch with a setting wide enough and long enough to capture at least three or four threads of the fabric in the stitching. Stitch as close to the edge as you can.

- **Overlock:** Many sewing machines offer one or more specialty stitches for overlocking the fabric's edge. These stitches combine a straight stitch and a stretch stitch. They are a bit more secure than a zigzag stitch and a little bulkier.

- **Serger:** A serger is designed for overlocking and produces a slightly neater and more secure finish. For a basic serged seam allowance, set the serger for a three-thread overlock stitch. If the fabric unravels particularly easily, use the widest setting.

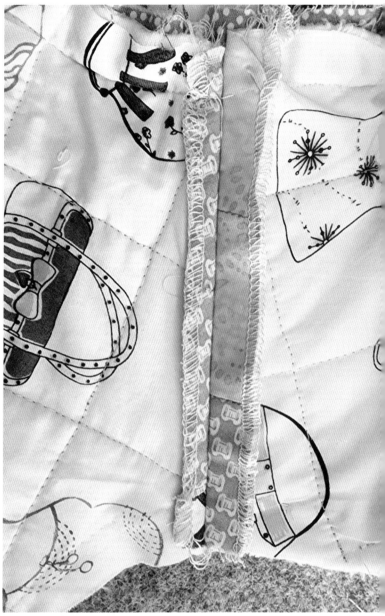

This seam allowance is pressed open and finished on each side with a serger.

Hong Kong Finish

A Hong Kong finish is an attractive and protective binding for seam allowances in a quilted jacket or coat. This finish is used on seam allowances that are pressed open and flat. We frequently finish shoulder seams with the Hong Kong technique to minimize bulk; if both seam allowances are pressed to the back before binding, they can produce an uncomfortable bump along the shoulder

Hong Kong Finish (cont.)

1. Cut bias binding strips at least 1" wide from the lining fabric, either a lightweight cotton or silky fabric. You will need enough bias strips to finish both raw edges of each seam allowance.

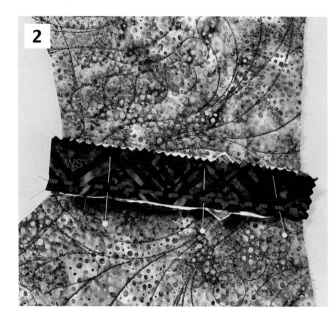

2. Place one raw edge of the bias strip against the raw edge of the seam allowance, right sides together. Stitch a ¼" seam connecting the binding strip to the edge of the seam allowance.

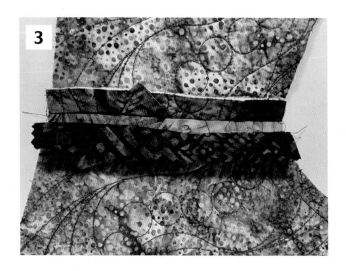

3. Press the binding strip away from the seam allowance.

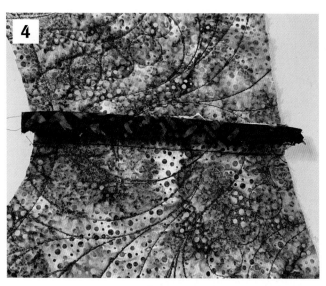

4. Wrap the binding around the edge of the seam allowance and press into place. The raw edge of the bias strip should be hidden between the seam allowance and the wrong side of the garment.

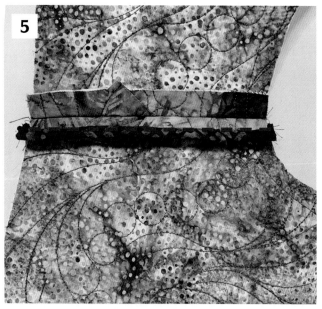

5. Stitch-in-the-ditch between the binding and the seam allowance to anchor the raw edge of the bias strip under the seam allowance. Repeat for remaining seam allowance.

Reversible Seam Binding

This type of bound seam completely encases a seam allowance with clean edges for seams that will be pressed to one side. It provides an attractive and secure decorative finish for seams in reversible garments. In these projects, Reversible Seam Binding is applied after the seam is stitched, batting is trimmed out of the seam allowances to reduce bulk, and the seam has been trimmed to ½" or graded as directed in the project.

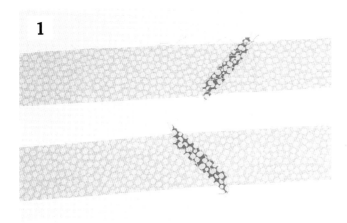

1. Measure the length of the seam to be bound, and cut a binding strip to the required length and width (see sidebar above). If needed, join multiple strips with angled seams along the grain to distribute the seam bulk along the

Reversible Seam Binding Width

Reversible Seam Binding is made with bias strips cut three times the width of the desired finished binding. For example, if covering a ½" wide seam allowance, the strips should be cut 1½" wide. If necessary, trim the seam allowances evenly to the desired width.

binding. Trim these seam allowances to ¼" and press open.

2. Press the jacket's seam allowances to be covered in the direction indicated in the project. Grade the seam allowances and trim the batting from the seam allowance. **Note:** When covering the seam that attaches the Opus Collar to the jacket's neckline, the seam allowances should be pressed toward the collar and will need to be clipped **at ½" intervals** to lay smoothly.

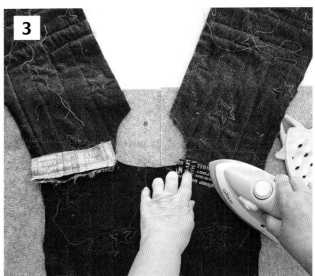

3. Unfold one-third of the binding and pin the raw edge to the seam allowances, right sides together. Stitch the binding in the fold along the stitched seam line. Press the binding toward the seam allowances. Wrap the binding around to cover the back of the seam and press in place.

4

4. Pin the binding fold to the garment and stitch it in place. While you can secure the loose edge of the binding to the garment by machine, we prefer to hand stitch the final seam for a less visible and more pliable finish.

Classic Binding Technique

Double-fold binding completely encases the raw edges of a quilted jacket or coat and provides an attractive finish to both the outside and inside of the garment. It can also be used to cover exposed seam allowances on the inside of a garment, as demonstrated in the Orphan Blocks Shirt Collar Jacket (page 68), but this technique does not lie flat like the Reversible Seam Binding technique. We generally prefer to cut the strips on the bias, but for applications with no curves, binding strips may be cut on the grain or cross grain.

Classic Binding Width

Classic Binding is made with strips cut four times the width of the desired finished binding. For example, if covering a ½" wide seam allowance, the strips should be cut 2" wide.

1. Measure the edge to be bound, and cut a binding strip the required length and width (see sidebar above). If needed, join multiple strips with angled seams along the fabric's grain to distribute the seam bulk along the binding. Trim the seam allowances to ¼" and press open.

2

2. Fold the binding strip in half the long way, wrong sides together, and press.

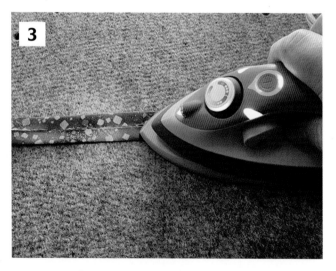

3

3. Press each side in half again, folding the raw edges just shy of the center, to set the binding. Try not to stretch bias strips while pressing.

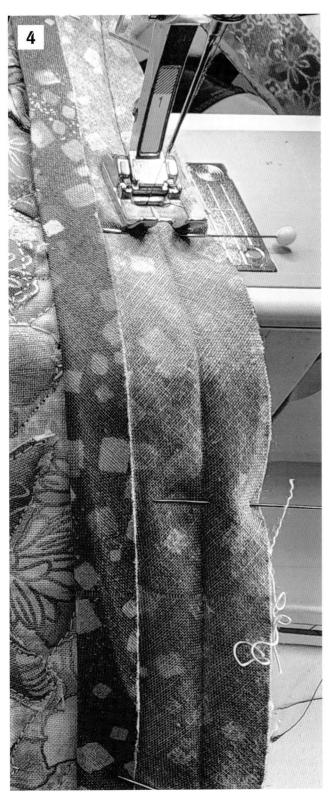

5. Press the binding toward the raw edge. Wrap the binding around so the center fold aligns with the garment edge and the second side of the binding covers the reverse side of the garment. The remaining fold of the binding should just cover the binding stitch line. Do not trim out the batting in the seam allowances. If needed to wrap the binding smoothly, trim the edge of all layers slightly.

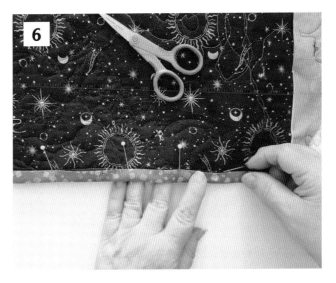

4. Unfold one edge and pin it right sides together along the edge to be bound. Stitch just inside the pressed fold to sew the binding to the section, backstitching at the beginning and end of the seam.

6. Press and then pin the binding smoothly in place. Stitch the loose edge to secure the binding on the second side. While it is quicker to stitch this on the machine, a visible straight line of stitching may not blend well with the

7

jacket's quilting style and produces a stiffer seam. We generally hand stitch the binding into place, burying the stitches into the layers of the quilted sections. Keep the stitches close together so the binding is secure.

7. When the binding needs to finish a raw edge at a corner, such as the Center Fronts at the collar edges and the hemline, add 1" for each corner when calculating the length of binding required. Leave 1" extending away from the corner when pinning the binding, but stop stitching the binding seam at the edge of the garment.

8. Unfold the binding extension and press it inside to cover the raw edge. Refold the binding and wrap it around to the reverse side for the Classic Binding Technique. Pin it in place and hand stitch the corner, carefully invisible stitching the end closed.

8

The Projects

Each project in this book explores a technique for designing and piecing the outer layer. The simplest "wholecloth" jackets feature a single fabric for each pattern section or for the entire jacket. The patchwork, Jelly Roll, and repurposed projects utilize a length of pieced fabric—perhaps you can use one made especially for this jacket or one from an unfinished quilt top or finished quilt. Several other projects explore methods of sectional piecing to integrate a central motif, a special panel, or orphan quilt blocks into a quilted jacket. In addition, we have chosen a quilting technique for each project that we feel complements the outer layer and have recommended an appropriate choice of batting and lining.

Choose one of the 10 projects in the book as your design direction or choose elements from several to combine into your personal coat project. Any piecing design or quilting technique can be applied to any size jacket or coat; any batting or lining selection can be used with any of the design options. Read more tips for planning your project in Design Guidelines (page 8) and Material Selection (page 10). Keep in mind that the projects are pictured in adult and kid sizes, but all designs can be customized to your body.

Wholecloth Jacket

Size Pictured: Adult Small

This wholecloth jacket with a front band is a great place to start making quilted jackets. By "wholecloth," we mean that each section of the jacket is cut from a single fabric without any piecing. All the sections can be cut from the same fabric or, like this sample, can be cut from a mixture of coordinating fabrics. This front band–style jacket is crafted from a group of coordinating fabrics, the Hibernation series produced by Tilda's World. An optional flat piping was used along the band to better tie the fabrics together.

MATERIALS NEEDED

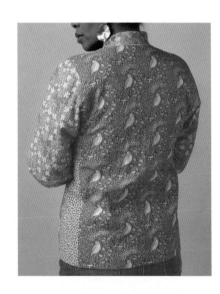

- Opus pattern, front band style, jacket length

- 1–1¾ yards of cotton print #1 (we used Sleepybird in Lafayette) for jacket's Front and Back

- 1–1¾ yards of cotton print #2 (we used Autumnbloom in Sage) for Sleeves and Band

- ½–1 yard of cotton print #3 (we used Eucalyptus in Lafayette) for Sides and *optional* flat bias piping

- 1½–2 yards of polyester fabric (we used 100% polyester in Eucalyptus) for lining

- Batting, as needed for the selected size (we used Quilters Dream Cotton)

- Thread (we used Sulky 30 wt. Cotton Blendables in 4021 Truly Teal) for quilting

- Polyester thread for construction, *optional*

- 3 large snaps

Design Features

- Each section of the jacket is free motion quilted with two layers: the outer layer and cotton batting.

- Free-hanging lining is inserted after construction of the quilted jacket.

- Snap closures are used as a finish.

- Front is finished with a 1½" wide quilted band and optional decorative flat piping.

Prepare and Quilt the Sections

1 Cut these jacket pattern pieces: Right Front, Left Front, and Back from print #1; Right Sleeve and Left Sleeve from print #2; Right Side and Left Side from print #3. Leave an extra ½" on all sides. Cut the same pieces from the batting, also with the extra ½" on the perimeter sides. Press each piece with steam iron.

2 For each jacket section, stack the outer layer fabric right side up on the batting. Press layers together with steam iron. Secure the two layers together for quilting by pinning or preferred method.

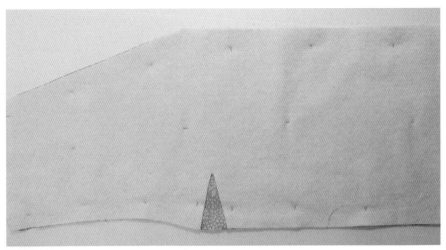

3 Mark darts on the back side of the batting on each Front; cut away batting between the dart legs.

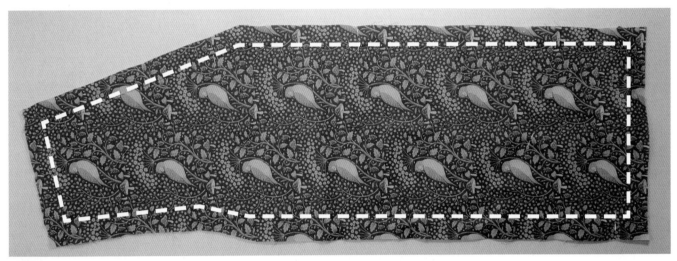

4 Use a straight-edge ruler and a disappearing marker (or preferred method) to draw a line 1" away from the edge of each section along the side seams, shoulder seams, neckline, and Center Front.

5 Make quilt sandwiches with your leftover fabric and batting scraps to test possible quilting techniques, quilting threads, and stitches before quilting the jacket sections.

6 Quilt each stacked section with preferred technique. As frequently as possible, start and stop stitching at the drawn lines with a few extra stitches in place to lock the threads. Prints #1 and #2 are free motion quilted by loosely following vine motifs. Print #3 is free motion quilted with wavy vertical lines.

7 Pull thread tails to the back side of each section and tie off if needed, especially where stitching was stopped or started inside the seam allowances. Press each section with a steam iron.

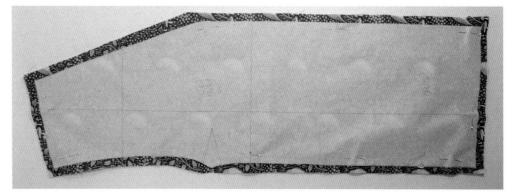

8 Lay each section on a table and re-pin the corresponding pattern piece to it. The pattern should be centered on the quilted jacket section with grain lines perpendicular to the hem. Make sure to look at the fronts together if your fabric's print needs to be aligned side to side.

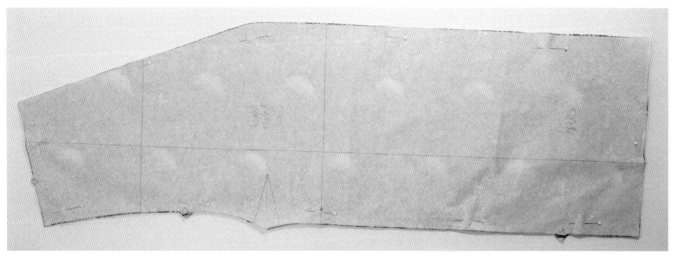

9 Cut away the excess fabric around the pattern piece, remembering to cut or mark the single and double notches on each section for easy construction. Transfer the markings for dots and darts to each prepared section.

Assemble the Jacket

This project closely follows the Construct the Opus Jacket or Coat steps 1–9 (page 27). We refer to those directions several times, but they are supplemented in this project.

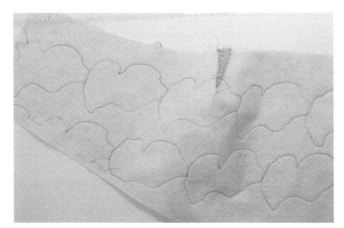

10 Sew and press the dart on each Front (step 1 of Construct).

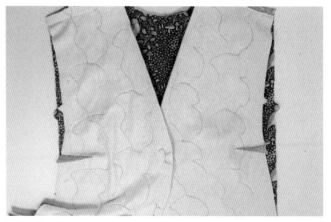

11 Pin and sew the Fronts and Back together at the shoulder seam (step 2 of Construct). Trim the batting from the seam allowances.

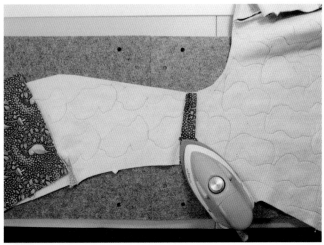

12 Press the seam allowances open. Because this jacket has a free-hanging lining, seam allowances do not require finishing; they will be concealed and protected by the lining.

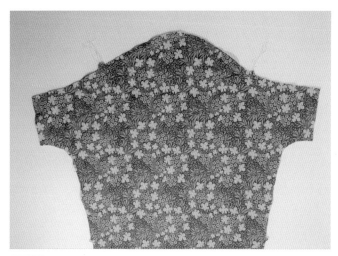

13 Stitch the optional gathering stitches between notches of the Sleeve head if desired.

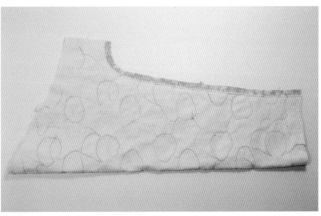

14 Sew the Sleeve underarm seam (step 3 of Construct). Trim the batting from the seam allowances, and clip the underarm curve.

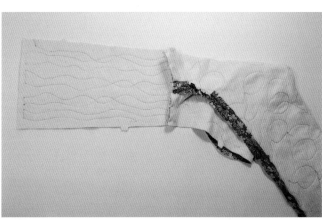

15 Press the underarm seam allowances open. Pin and sew each Sleeve to its corresponding Side (step 4 of Construct). Trim the batting from the seam allowances and press the seam open.

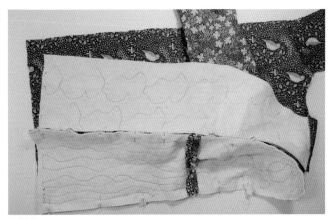

16 Pin one Sleeve/Side unit into the body of the jacket (step 5 of Construct), matching notches. Pin from the armhole notches to the hem in the back and front.

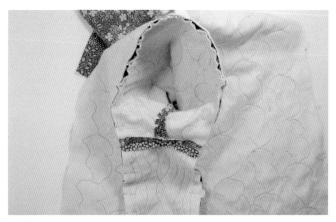

17 Pin the Sleeve dot to the shoulder seam. Continue pinning to the notches, pulling the gather threads as needed to ease the Sleeve head into the armhole.

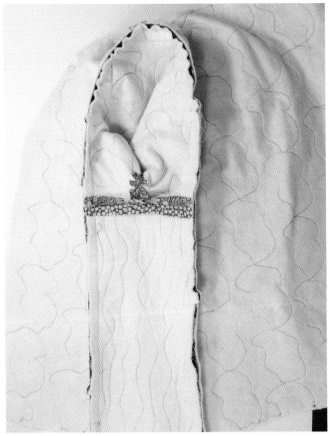

19 Repeat steps 16–18 for a second Sleeve/Side unit.

20 Try the jacket on right side out. Fronts should just meet at the Center Front. If desired, make fitting adjustments at this point and note the changes on your pattern pieces (step 6 of Construct).

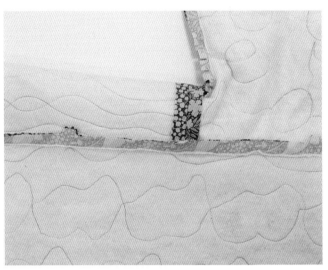

18 Sew the Side seam from one hem around the shoulder to the other hem with basting stitches (step 5 of Construct). Check the work for caught fabric and make corrections if needed.

21 When satisfied with the fit, re-sew Side seams with standard-length stitches. Trim the batting from the seam allowances along the Side seams. Press both seam allowances toward the Sleeve/Side unit.

Add the Optional Flat Piping

If not adding the optional flat piping to your project, skip to the next section, Hem the Jacket and Sleeves.

22 Measure the total length of the seam into which you are inserting the piping—from the bottom of the Right Front, around the neckline, to the bottom of the Left Front—and add 2" for ease. This jacket features a ⅜" wide strip of piping, so the strips are cut 2" wide (⅝" seam allowance + ⅜" visible piping x 2).

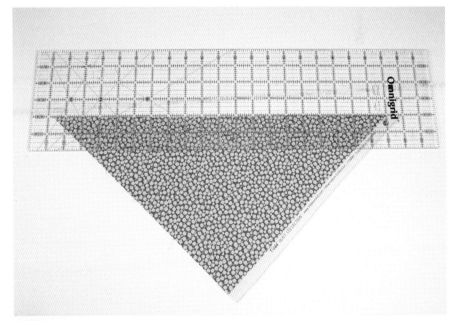

23 Cut enough strips of print #3 to create the total length of piping, accounting for the seams required to join strips. Cut the piping strips on the bias if possible, but if you don't have enough fabric, you can get away with cutting the strips on the straight of grain.

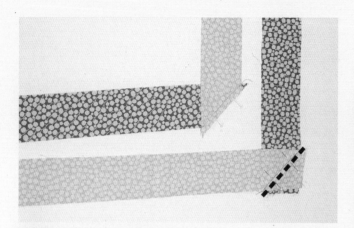

24 Sew the piping strips right sides together on the diagonal.

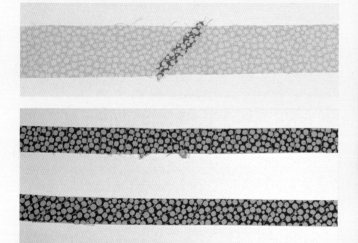

25 Trim the seam allowance to ¼" and press seams open. Press the entire piping strip in half the long way, wrong sides together.

26 Pin piping to the right side of the jacket, matching the unfinished edges. Start pinning at the center Back, easing gently around the neckline curves, and work toward the hems. Machine baste the piping into place ⅜" from the folded edge of the piping.

Hem the Jacket and Sleeves

27 Try the jacket on again to mark the desired length of the sleeves and body of the jacket with pins or a removable-marking method. Trim away the fabric that extends beyond the 1½" needed to turn up the hem (step 7 of Construct). Stitch along the raw edges with a straight or zigzag stitch to prevent fraying.

28 Press and pin the hems up 1½" along the bottom edge of the jacket and each sleeve. Stitch the hems in place by hand or by machine with topstitching.

Insert the Free-Hanging Lining

29 Cut out the lining fabric: two Fronts, one full Back, two Sides, and two Sleeves. Assemble the lining following Construct the Opus Jacket or Coat steps 1–5.

30 Lay the quilted jacket on a table right side out. Turn the lining wrong side out and insert it into the quilted jacket. The lining will be longer than the hemmed jacket. Pin the lining to the jacket along the front edge (step 8 of Construct). Baste, stopping 4" from the hem on both the Right and Left Front.

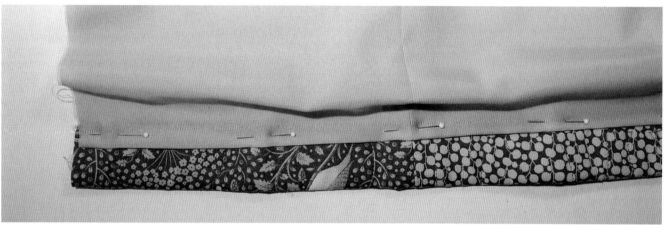

31 Trim the lining to ½" longer than the hemmed jacket and sleeves. Fold and press the raw edge of lining to the wrong side by ½". Pin the pressed edge of the lining to the jacket hem and sleeves, just covering the raw edge of the finished hem.

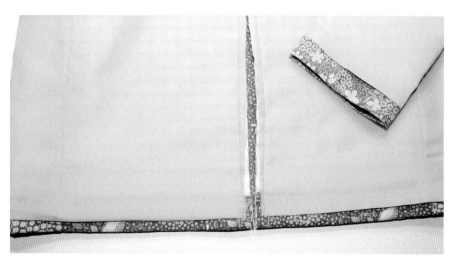

32 Hand stitch the lining to the hem using a slip stitch or your preferred stitch. Press the lining toward hem so the excess fold (jump) lies flat against the hem. Finish basting the lining to the Center Front of the jacket, securing the jump.

33 Try on the jacket, hang it on a hanger, or place on a dress form to make sure the lining does not hang below the hem. Correct if necessary.

Add the Front Band and Closures

34 Calculate the length needed for front Band (step 9 of Construct). From print #2, cut two rectangular Band pieces 4¼" wide x the calculated length. This will create a 1½" wide finished Band. Cut two rectangular pieces of batting the same length x 2⅜" wide. Secure batting to one long edge of each Band with easily removable basting stitches, pins, or spray adhesive. The batting should extend ¼" over the center of each Band.

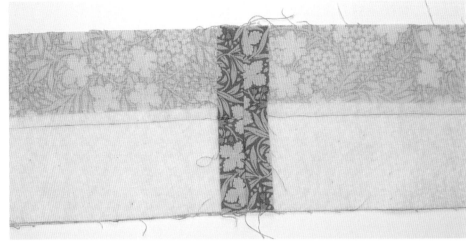

35 Stitch the Band pieces together along one short side with a ⅝" seam, backstitching at the beginning and end. Trim the batting from the seam allowances and press the seam open. Press Band in half lengthwise, wrong sides together.

36 Open the Band. Pin the side with batting to the jacket's edge. Match the Band's center-back seam to the jacket's center back, and pin toward the hems (step 9 of Construct). The Band should be 1" longer than each jacket front.

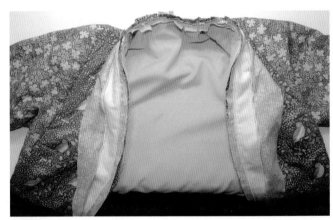

37 Sew the Band with ⅝" seam. Check for mistakes and correct if needed. Trim the batting from the seam allowances and clip curves around the neck and shoulders. If the optional piping was added, trim off ¼"–⅜" of the piping seam allowances. Press all seam allowances toward the Band.

38 Fold and press the long raw edge of the Band under by ⅝", toward the wrong side. Fold the loose ends of Band up to the jacket hem length and press.

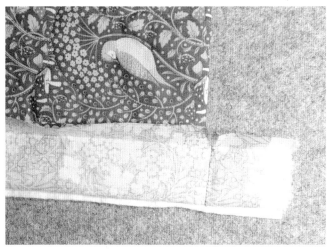

39 Open the pressed Band. At the front hem, reverse fold the end of the Band right sides together, and stitch just below pressed fold from the outer edge to the ⅝" seam line. Turn the Band to the right side to make sure the bottom of the Band lines up with the jacket hem. Correct placement of stitch line if they do not line up.

40 Turn the Band wrong side out again to trim off excess fabric below stitching line, leaving about ¼". Clip the corner to reduce bulk.

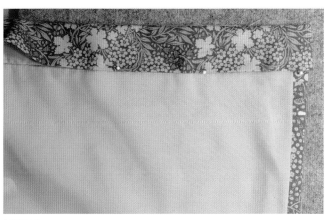

41 Turn the Band right side out, re-pressing along the center fold made in step 35. Pin the pressed edge of the Band to the inside of the jacket along the seam line. Hand stitch the Band to the lining along the seam line using a slip stitch or your preferred stitch.

42 Quilt the finished Band with your choice of quilting techniques. Try to stop and start as little as possible, as you will need to tie off and bury all the thread tails between the layers.

43 Try the jacket on to determine the placement of the three large snaps. Mark the location for each snap on both front Bands with pins. Lay the jacket on a table with the hems aligned to make sure the snap placement is correct on both front Bands. Sew the snaps on and wear your fabulous, quilted jacket!

Jelly Roll and Appliqué Coat

Size Pictured: Adult Medium

Fabric strips are given life and interest in this asymmetrical design. The back pattern is divided to feature stripes running horizontally and vertically. Star appliqués can be added after quilting but before construction to create a simple scene. Customize this formula for yourself in any combination of Jelly Roll strips and decorative appliqués.

The fabric for the fronts and backs was created from two sets of precut Jelly Roll strips in cotton batik. They are available from quilting vendors in a wide variety of fabrics. This coat features an extra wide front band, 3" finished width, which creates the appearance of a shawl collar. It is also wide enough to support appliqués if desired.

MATERIALS NEEDED

- Opus pattern, front band style, coat length, basic sleeve length

- 2–3 Jelly Rolls of cotton fabric (we used SewBatik) for pieced Fronts and Back

- 1 ¼–1 ½ yards of coordinating cotton fabric (we used SewBatik) for Sleeves

- 1 ¼ yards of coordinating cotton fabric (we used SewBatik) for Sides and front Band

- ¼ yard of contrasting fabric (we used Batik Gradations from SewBatik) for star appliqués, optional

- 2–3 yards of silky fabric (we used China silk) for lining

- 1 package of double-sided light fusible web (we used Lite Steam-A-Seam 2®) for star appliqués, optional

- Batting, as needed for the selected size (we used Quilters Dream Dream Black Poly)

- Thread (we used Sulky 30 wt. Cotton Blendables in 4022 Midnight Sky) for quilting

- Thread (we used Gutermann TERA 80) for construction

- 5 buttons at least 1" wide

Design Features

- **Fabric for the Fronts and Back are pieced together from precut Jelly Roll strips.**

- **The back pattern is divided slightly off center to create design interest with the direction of the stripes.**

- **Appliqués are added for thematic design interest.**

- **Decorative, mismatched buttons; the wide band can accommodate large buttons.**

- **The front band is 3" wide to create a cozy faux-shawl collar.**

Prepare the Patterns

1 Cut out two Front patterns and label the Right Front for vertical stripes and the Left Front for horizontal stripes.

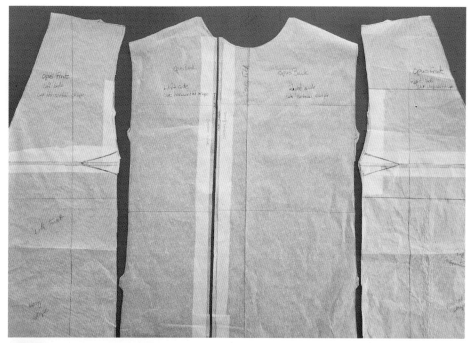

2 Cut out a full Back pattern. Measure 2" to the right of the center fold, and draw a line from the neckline to the hem, parallel to the center-back fold line. Cut the pattern along this line and label the Right Back (wider portion) for vertical stripes and Left Back for horizontal stripes. Add a ¼" seam allowance along both the Right and Left Back where the pattern was cut apart.

Create the Outer Layer

3 Arrange the Jelly Roll strips in the order to sew them. As you consider which colors you want to highlight, keep in mind that the Fronts and Backs will be cut around the perimeter of the pieced fabric.

Tip

Place a few pins along the seam before sewing strips together to prevent getting mixed up about which raw edge of the strips to join.

4 Stitch the long edges of the strips together one at a time with ¼" seam allowances. Set each seam by pressing it from the wrong side, then press the pieced fabric open with both seam allowances to one side. Consistently press all seam allowances in the same direction. When all strips are joined, press well again from the right side of the pieced fabric.

5 Place the patterns along the horizontal or vertical stripes of the fabric, as labeled. Position the pattern pieces to enhance your desired design on the Jelly Roll fabric; the purple strips are placed most prominently on this coat. Leave enough space between the patterns to add ½" around all perimeter sides. Do not add the extra ½" along the Backs where they were divided. Cut out the Front and Back sections.

6 Pin the two Back fabric sections along the dividing line, right sides together. Sew with a ¼" seam allowance so the final vertical stripe will be 2" wide like the others. Press both seam allowances toward the vertical stripes.

Prepare the Layers

7 Cut two Sleeves and two Sides from their respective coordinating fabric, adding 1/2" all around each piece.

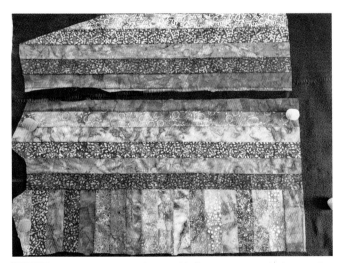

8 Use patterns, or each assembled section, to cut the batting for two Fronts, two Sleeves, two Sides, and one full Back. If using pattern pieces, add ½" around perimeter to accommodate quilt shrinkage. Remove the batting from each dart before quilting.

9 Stack each outer layer, right side up, on top of the corresponding batting piece. Press the two layers together. Anchor the batting and fabric together with pins or by preferred method.

Quilt the Coat Sections

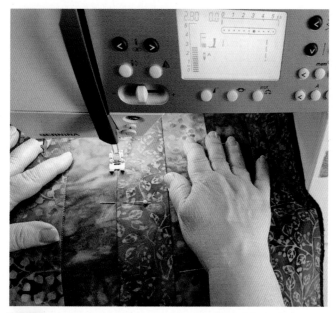

10 The Fronts and Back are easily quilted by stitching-in-the-ditch between each strip. Remember to leave 1" unquilted on all sides to be able to trim the batting from the seam allowances after quilting. Mark the stopping point before sewing if helpful.

11 Each Sleeve and Side section is stitched with straight quilting lines 2" apart to mimic the pieced Jelly Roll sections. The dark fabric was marked with lines using a chalk roller and ruler. Alternatively, a guide bar could be added to the machine for spacing.

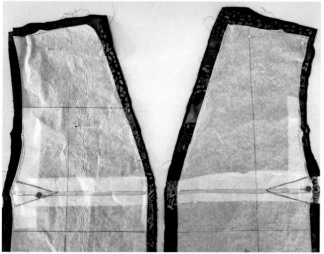

12 Press each section well. Place the corresponding pattern on each section to cut to the correct size, trimming away excess fabric. Be sure to align the pattern to the cut-out dart sections before trimming.

Add the Star Appliqués

If not adding the optional appliqués to your project, skip to the next section, Construct Coat and Lining.

13 Sketch out a design for the coat to estimate how many stars you will need. This coat features 3 large, 9 medium, 14 small, and 22 extra-small stars plus 19 small diamonds cut from scraps. Consider connecting the Right and Left Fronts with a few appliqués on the right side of the front Band.

14 Back the fabric or fabric scraps with double-sided fusible web to allow for consistency of shape and to maintain the star shape when applied to the coat. Cut stars out with a die cutter or by hand (see the sidebar Make Your Own Appliqués).

15 Peel away the layer of paper so the back of the appliqué is tacky. Place all appliqués at least ¾" away from the edge of each section, so they will not be caught in a seam allowance, and place strategically in the bust area. Consider how the sections will fit together. Walk away and revisit to check the placement. If available, pin the Front and Back sections onto a dress form to see the appliqués in three dimensions.

16 When satisfied with the placement, fuse each star into place, and then quilt them using the chosen method. On this coat, the stars are stitched on with a technique that resembles a pie cut into pieces. Echo quilting provides a halo around each star approximately ¼" away from the appliqué.

Make Your Own Appliqués

1. Create the pattern by tracing the shapes you want onto copy paper and darkening the pattern lines.

2. Determine which is the easiest side of the double-sided medium to peel the paper away, and then turn the medium over.

3. Place the pattern under this flipped medium, and trace the patterns onto the medium.

4. Peel away the undrawn side and attach it to the wrong side of the desired fabric. Press gently.

5. Carefully cut the appliqués out following the drawn lines.

6. It is easier to work with small sections of fabric and medium, rather than tracing a large number of stars on a large piece of medium.

Construct Coat and Lining

17 Assemble the coat following Construct the Opus Jacket or Coat steps 1–5 (page 27). Trim the batting away from inside each seam allowance at each step of construction, pressing well after each step.

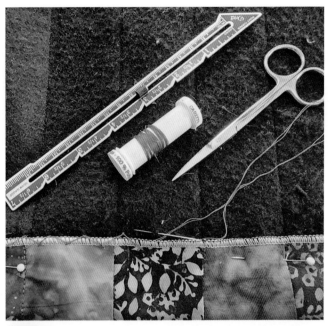

18 Hem the coat and sleeves (step 7 of Construct). This coat has a 1½" deep turned-up hem on the body and 1¼" deep sleeve hems. Hems are secured with hand stitching.

19 Prepare and insert the lining into the coat (step 8 of Construct). Tack the lining to the coat with loose stitches or a thread chain under the armhole and at the shoulder point. Hand stitch the hem of the lining to the coat with a jump pleat.

Add Wide Front Band and Buttons

20 Measure the length from the center back of the neckline to the finished hem and add 2". Cut two Bands along the grain line of the band fabric 7¼" wide x the calculated length. Stitch the two Band pieces together at the center back (step 9 of Construct). Press the seam open and press the Band in half along the full length, wrong sides together.

21 Cut two batting pieces 3½" wide x the calculated Band length. Position the batting pieces on the wrong side of the Band ¼" away from one raw edge. Machine or hand baste the batting to the Band with a ½" seam allowance.

If not adding the optional appliqués to your project, skip to step 24.

22 Baste the batting side of the Band in place on the right side of the coat, matching the center-back seam of the Band to the center back of the coat. Ease the Band along the curved neck edges and along the shaped Front through the chest, matching the pieces along the ⅝" seam line. Press lightly and position appliqués to connect the design on the Right and Left Fronts of the coat. Consider the button closures when placing the appliqués.

23 Remove the Band and stitch on the appliqués using the same method used on the coat.

24 Pin the batting side of the Band around the coat opening along the ⅝" seam line, matching the center-back Band seam to the center-back neck. Sew, easing gently into the curve around the neck and along the bend in each center front neckline. Press well and assess placement for a smooth application and accurate appliqué placement.

25 Trim away the batting from the seam allowances. Re-press the center fold of the Band, incorporating the extra ¼" of batting into the crease. Press the raw edge of the Band under ⅝" so it can easily be tacked over the Band's seam.

26 Finish the hem of the Band (step 9 of Construct). Turn the Band right side out to check the seams, and once satisfied, grade and trim the seam allowances.

27 Press the Band flat. Pin the inside edge of the Band over the seam that joins it to the coat. Hand stitch the inside edge of the Band down securely, and then press the entire Band again.

28 Quilt the finished Band. This band was stitched in a straight line ⅜" from the seam on each long edge to mirror the 2" wide quilting lines on the coat.

29 Position the buttons 3" apart on the left side of the Band. Vertical buttonholes were worked on the machine to align with the button positioning.

Assorted Patchwork Jacket

Size Pictured: Adult Large

In this project, we are creating a piece of patchwork fabric for each jacket section. Working in sections this way permits better design control and reduces waste. They can be cut from favorite fabrics in your stash, as this sample is, from a specially purchased set of fabrics, or from precut Charm Packs. Alternatively, create one large piece of patchwork fabric, as was done in the Jelly Roll and Appliqué Coat, then cut the pattern pieces out of the fabric.

Because the lining is quilted into this jacket, binding the end of each sleeve allows for a tidy finish that can be rolled back into a cuff, perfect for this colorful and lightweight jacket.

MATERIALS NEEDED

- Opus pattern, front band style, jacket length, turn-back cuff sleeve length

- (110) 5" x 5" squares of fabric or as needed for the selected size

- ½ yard of fabric for Sides

- ½ yard of fabric for front Band and sleeve bindings

- Cotton lining fabric, as needed for the selected size

- Batting, as needed for the selected size (we used Hobbs Heirloom® Premium Cotton Batting)

- Thread (we used Sulky 30 wt. Cotton Blendables) for quilting

- Thread (we used Gutermann TERA 80) for construction

- Buttons, optional

- Scrap fabric for loops, optional

Design Features

- Sleeves are pieced before quilting, in addition to the Fronts and Back.

- A quilted-in cotton lining with appropriate seam finishes.

- Narrow ⅝" front band finish.

- Binding to finish the sleeve hem for a turn-back cuff.

- Button and loop closure.

Create the Fabric

1 Gather cut squares for your patchwork jacket, keeping in mind that fabrics of similar colors and scales work well together. Ideally, each fabric will appear more than once. Have more squares than you will need for making design choices.

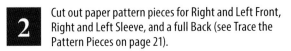

2 Cut out paper pattern pieces for Right and Left Front, Right and Left Sleeve, and a full Back (see Trace the Pattern Pieces on page 21).

3 Arrange the precut squares on each of the five pattern pieces, overlapping them ½" at each join, to achieve a pleasing look and make a realistic plan. Make each section at least ½" larger than the actual pattern along all sides.

4 Note that the patchwork fabric assembled for each sleeve features a row of three offset blocks at the top and two extra blocks to either side to accommodate the shape of the sleeve pattern without creating much waste.

5 Stitch the squares together using a ¼" seam. Press the seam allowances together and to one side, alternating sides to distribute the bulk. Keep section joins as small as possible; perhaps assemble groups of four blocks, then join them together, pressing after sewing each seam.

Rae's Tips for Garment Stitchers

If you do not have a ¼" foot, which is often used by quilters, find a needle position and mark on your machine. Or apply painter's tape to guide the ¼" seam allowance. (The ¼" seam looks impossibly small to a sewer accustomed to a ⅝" seam!)

It is also helpful to build the fabric in small groups, then connect the groups, pinning things together using a consistent system. I always fold the fabrics left over right, and pin the actual seam line before heading to the sewing machine. Marking with a pin or chalk the top of the left block also assists in future layers of assembly.

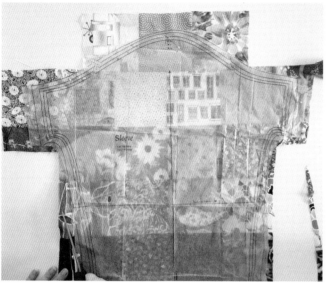

6 Once each fabric section has been assembled and pressed, lay the corresponding pattern piece on top of it, and pin or weight it in place. Cut the fabric into the correct shape, adding an extra ½" on all sides.

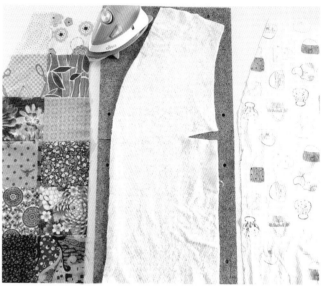

7 Cut the batting and the lining using the same pattern pieces and the same technique of adding ½" on all sides. Use a marking tool to mark the darts on the right side of the lining and on the batting.

8 Assemble the quilt sandwiches for each jacket section with the lining right side down, batting in the center, and pieced fabric right side facing up. Press each layer again before stacking. Once the three layers are stacked, press the entire sandwich well, beginning in the center and radiating out. Press the stack from both the lining side and the piecing side.

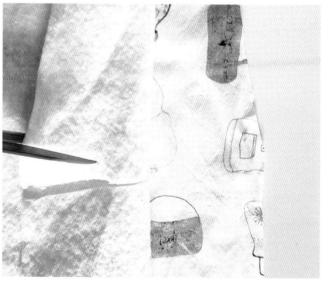

9 For each pattern piece with darts, lay the pattern back on its section and make sure the dart markings are aligned on all three layers. Adjust if needed, then cut away only the batting between the dart legs. This minimizes bulk when the dart is stitched into place. You will quilt as if it is still there.

Assorted Patchwork Jacket **63**

Quilt the Sections

10 Pin each stacked sandwich to keep the layers aligned while quilting each section. Follow the piecing lines vertically and horizontally for your first set of quilting stitches. Don't forget to stop stitching 1" from each edge and to backstitch lightly. Press after these stitching lines are finished.

11 If desired, add a second set of quilting stitches to divide each square into four equal sections. Mark quilting lines with a tested, easy-to-remove marker or use a guide bar to stitch straight lines. On this jacket, the 5" x 5" squares become 4½" x 4½" squares when pieced, so the second set of quilting lines are 2¼" away from the piecing lines.

12 Once the quilting is completed, press the sandwich again on each side and check for any bumps or irregularities in the quilting that should be corrected before continuing.

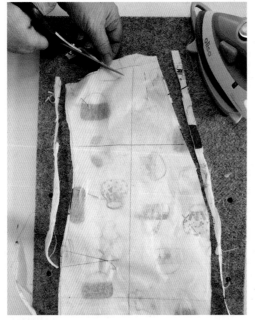

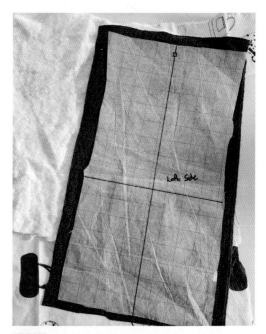

13 Lay the pattern piece on the section and trim away any excess fabric around the edges. Lay the two Fronts side by side before trimming to make sure they are aligned correctly. Don't forget to cut or mark the single and double notches on each section.

14 Prepare the Side panels following the same process: cut the two Sides out of the primary, batting, and lining fabrics; stack; press the layers, and quilt. In this sample, the sides are quilted with the same 2¼" grid of quilting stitches. Lay the pattern back on each Side section and trim away any excess fabric, marking or cutting the single and double notches.

Construct the Jacket

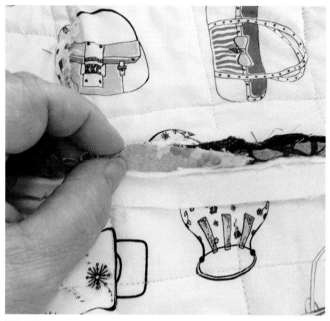

15 Assemble the jacket, following Construct the Opus Jacket or Coat steps 1–5 (page 27). Trim the batting away from inside each seam allowance at each step of construction, pressing well after each step.

16 Finish the jacket's seams and hem edges. In this sample, we used a three-thread overlock on a serger, but a zigzag or overlock stitch on a sewing machine will also work. If you prefer hand finishes, a hand overcast or blanket stitch will make a beautiful finish too.

Finish Sleeve with Binding

17 Measure the circumference of the sleeve hem and add 1" for a ½" seam allowance.

18 Cut two bias strips of the desired fabric the calculated length by 2½" wide. Press each strip in half the long way, and then press the two halves into the centerfold. Stitch the short ends of each binding strip together with a ½" seam to create a circle; repress the creases along the fold line. Cutting the seams along the straight grain is the best option.

19 Check that the binding matches the sleeve circumference, and adjust if it is larger than the sleeve hem. Excess binding creates a lumpy finish. Open the folded seam allowance along the binding's top edge as you slide it onto the sleeve, right sides together. Pin the opened edge along the raw edges of the quilted sleeve, positioning the binding seam near the sleeve seam. Stitch along the crease line for a ⅝" seam allowance.

20 Press the binding toward the sleeve hem, and then wrap the binding to the lining side. Do not grade the seam or trim out the batting in this seam; it will fill the binding nicely. On the lining side, pin the binding to cover the seam stitches. Hand stitch the folded binding edge neatly over the seamline. Press gently to set the binding.

Add the Narrow Center Front Band

21 Calculate the length needed for front Band (step 9 of Construct). Cut two rectangular Band pieces 3 ¼" wide x the calculated length. This will create a 1" wide finished Band. While this pattern is designed for the Band to be cut on the straight of grain, this narrow Band can be cut on the bias if preferred. There is no need to interface or put batting in this Band.

22 Apply the front Band (step 9 of Construct). Do not grade the seam or remove the batting from the seam allowances. These extra layers will provide the filler needed to keep the Band balanced with the jacket.

23 If you are adding buttons and loops to the jacket opening, follow the directions in the sidebar (page 67) to make, place, and attach the loops.

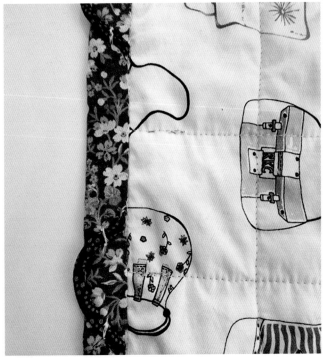

24 Finish the bottom and inside edge of the jacket Band with hand stitches (step 9 of Construct). Press the loops across the Band, and hand tack them securely to all but the outer layer of the Band.

Tip

These barely seen loops create a very secure closure, anchoring the Band together naturally. Larger, floppier loops are not as effective at keeping the jacket closed neatly around a medium- to large-size button.

Add Buttons and Loops to a Narrow Band

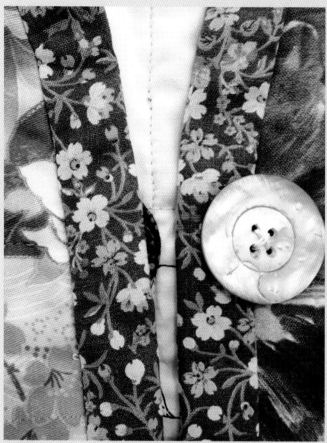

23a Choose the buttons and determine their placement; here, three vintage, same-size shell buttons were attached at regular intervals along the existing quilting lines. The buttons are stitched to the Left Front of the jacket and the loops placed on the Right Front.

23b Determine the length of the loops by measuring the diameter of the button and doubling that number. Make a sample to determine the required size of the loops so they slide smoothly, but not loosely, around the buttons. Cut bias strips 1" wide by the loop length or longer.

23c Stitch the strips into tubes using a ¼" seam. Turn them right side out with a preferred tube turner. Shorter strips are easier to turn. Lightly press each loop into a half-moon shape.

23d Pin loops on the center-front opening so a loop straddles each button placement. Fold the band into place to test the size and shape of the loops, making sure that the buttons will sit on top of the finished Band. When satisfied, stitch the loops in place where each end crosses the Band seam line.

Orphan Blocks Shirt Collar Jacket

Size Pictured: Adult Small

This jacket and its companion (page 104) incorporate quilt blocks from an unfinished quilt project. We hope you'll view this project as an inspiration and guide to creating a quilted jacket with your own stash of unfinished or orphaned blocks. We collected fabrics, both modern and vintage, that complemented the fabric in the original orphan blocks.

Two of the orphan blocks are featured prominently as front pockets and others are incorporated into the back and sleeves with traditional quilt sashing and piecing techniques. The roll back hems of the sleeves are also faced with an orphan block and additional cotton scraps.

MATERIALS NEEDED

- Opus pattern, shirt collar style, jacket length, roll back cuff

- (5) 6" x 6" quilt blocks or as needed for Back and pockets

- (2) 5" x 5" quilt blocks or as needed for cuffs

- 1½–2 yards of vintage cotton floral fabric for Upper Back and Fronts, Sleeves, and front facings

- 1–1½ yards of blue quilting cotton for Lower Back and Fronts, Sides, and Collar

- ½–1 yard of yellow quilting cotton for binding edges of jacket

- ¼ yard or collected scraps for the underside of the Collar and sashing

- 2–3 yards of silky fabric (we used Bemberg rayon), for lining

- Batting, as needed for the selected size (we used Quilters Dream Bamboo)

- Thread (we used Aurifil Cotton 40 wt.) for quilting

- Thread (we used Gutermann Mara 80) for construction

- 5 buttons at most 1½" wide

Design Features

- Dividing pattern pieces to create upper and lower Fronts and Back.

- Sashing to incorporate orphan blocks.

- Patch pockets on Front.

- Quilted-in silky lining.

- Facings at Center Front and roll back cuffs.

- Seam allowances bound with a variety of finishing techniques.

- Jacket edges finished with the Classic Binding Technique.

- Buttons are used as the closures.

Prepare the Patterns

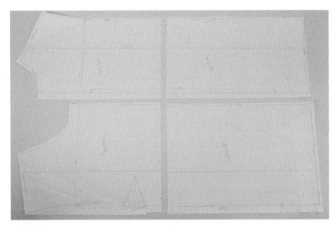

1 Trace a Front pattern and full Back pattern onto tissue paper, including the grainlines, horizontal balance lines, and all markings. Cut each traced pattern in two along the middle horizontal balance line. Label the pieces Upper Front, Lower Front, Upper Back, and Lower Back. Do **not** add a seam allowance or extra ½" for quilting shrinkage along these sides.

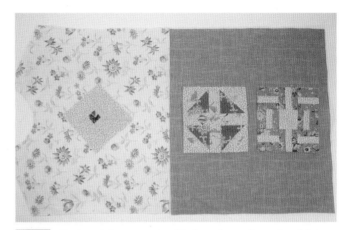

2 Contemplate your orphan blocks and complementary fabrics to plan the design. Read the sidebar below about fabric. The number and size of your blocks will be a significant factor, as well as how prominently you wish to feature them. The repetition of the same fabrics on the Fronts, Back, Sleeves, and Sides will help to bring it all together.

Mixing Vintage and Modern Fabrics

The orphan quilt blocks in this project were made with fabric from several years ago. This meant they did not match fabrics currently in quilt stores. The color gradations and shades were off just enough that we reached out to a cherished friend and vintage fabric expert in France. She helped us find the soft, sweet, slightly faded colors that blended with the older blocks. How can you do the same?

- Check your stash, and maybe friends, for fabrics that are not in new collections. Even if there are only small scraps, they can provide the jump between a new and old fabric.

- Visit stores that have been selling fabric for years, which might have some older shades.

- Visit vintage and consignment stores looking for garments made in fabric that will coordinate.

- Consider hand-dyed fabrics, batiks, and quilt blenders that have more nuanced colors.

- Try not to be in a hurry. Carry the orphan fabric or block along with you whenever you shop for fabric. One day, the perfect match will come along.

What is the next step?

- Test vintage fabrics for durability by tugging them in several directions to see if they tear

easily. It is best not to use fabrics that are rotten or deteriorating. If there is a sentimental fabric that is problematic, consider interfacing or underlining it to support it in the project.

- Prewash the fabrics or garments in the way you anticipate cleaning the coat or jacket.

- To remove stains or other discoloration, soak the fabric in a solution of nonchlorine bleach or enzyme cleaner with a gentle detergent. Machine wash on gentle cycle in cool water and lay in the sun to dry if possible.

- If there are still some spots or discoloration, try some additional wash cycles or plan your fabric layout to avoid these sections.

Build the Orphan Blocks

Front Pockets

These front pockets were built on a fabric foundation for stability. An alternative method would be to build out the orphan block to desired size, then quilt it to a batting foundation.

3 Cut two squares of batting, muslin, or other foundation fabric on which to build the pocket. This foundation should be at least 3" wider and taller than the orphan block; excess will be cut away later. Center each orphan block on one square; pin or baste the block in place.

4 Surround the block with one to three layers of sashing. Think about the pocket size, how it will look relative to the jacket size, and the fabrics or colors you want to bring into the Front to coordinate with the Back blocks. These sashes can be cut on the straight of grain, cross grain, or on the bias. Follow these steps to apply each layer of sashing:

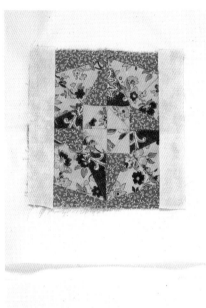

4a Sew a 1" wide strip to two opposite sides of the orphan block with ¼" seams. Press the strips away from the block. Trim ends even with the other sides of the orphan block.

4b Sew a 1" wide strip to the other two opposite sides of the orphan block with ¼" seams. Press the strips away from the block. Trim ends even with the other sides of the orphan block.

4c Repeat as many times as desired. Position the pockets on the jacket as you go to assess their size and whether more layers of sashing are desired. Trim away excess foundation fabric, squaring up the block. Measure its length and width.

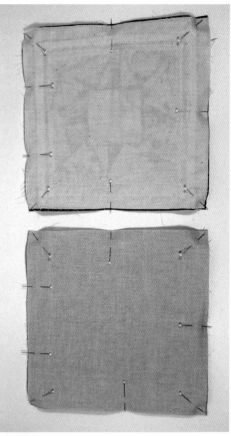

5 Cut two squares of backing fabric to the measured size of the sashed orphan blocks. If the foundation was not batting, apply a square of fusible interfacing to the wrong side of the backing squares for support.

6 Pin the backing to orphan block, right sides together, and sew with a ¼" seam. Leave 3" open (unsewn) on one side of the square.

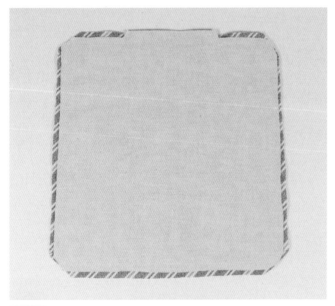

7 Trim the seam allowances to reduce bulk and clip across the corners.

8 Turn the pocket right side out through the opening. Press the pocket, pressing the seam allowances of the opening to the inside.

Back Blocks

The back blocks do not require a foundation because they will be quilted into the back section of the jacket.

9 Follow step 4 to add sashing to the orphan blocks. They are joined together by a sash, and a piece of blue cotton was added at the bottom to make the unit the same length as the Lower Back pattern with an extra ½" for quilting shrinkage. Cut two sashes 1" wide x the length of the orphan block unit. Stitch to each side and press away from the unit.

10 Follow step 4 to add narrow sashing to the orphan block for the upper back. The binding on the appliqué block is applied in a continuous strip like a quilt binding, but the raw edge (pressed to the wrong side of the block) is unfinished to reduce bulk.

Piece the Outer Layer

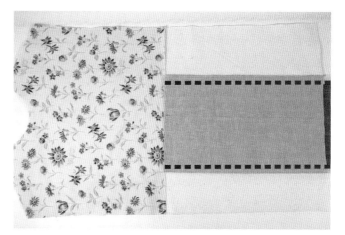

11 Cut Upper Fronts, Upper Back, and Sleeves from the vintage floral cotton. Cut the Lower Fronts and Sides from the modern blue cotton. Remember to cut ½" larger around the perimeter of each section. Do not add the extra ½" where the Front and Back patterns were split.

12 Lay the orphan unit on the center of the Lower Back pattern to calculate additional width needed on both sides to complete the full Lower Back; add ¾" to the measured width. Cut two pieces of blue cotton to the required width x Lower Back length. Stitch the pieces to the framing sash with a ¼" seam. Press the seam allowance toward the sash.

13 Measure the width of the full Upper Back and each Upper Front along the horizontal balance line. Cut framing sashes 1" wide x the measured length for the Back and both Fronts.

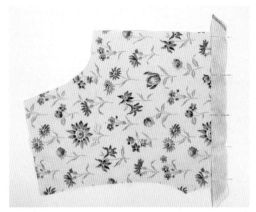

14 Stitch sashes to Upper Fronts and Upper Back with a ¼" seam. Press sashes away from the upper portions.

15 Pair the Lower Fronts and Lower Back with their upper counterparts. Stitch to the other side of the sashes with ¼" seams. Press so that the seam allowance fills the sash.

Prepare Lining and Batting Layers

The Opus shirt collar style shows the quilted-in lining where the front opens below the collar and the cuff. This jacket has facings applied on top of the linging fabric to match the outer layer. If not adding the optional facing, skip to the next section, Stack and Quilt the Jacket Sections.

16 Use the Opus pattern pieces or pieced outer layers to cut a full set of jacket pieces from the batting and the lining fabric. Cut ½" larger on all sides.

Front Facings

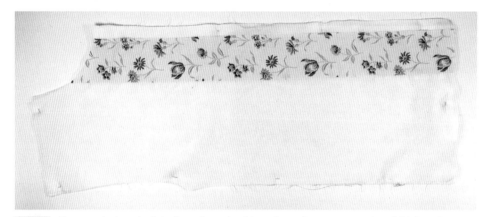

17 Measure the length of the Front from shoulder to hem. Cut two rectangles of this length x 3¾"–4" wide from the vintage floral fabric. Clean finish the inner edge of the facing. Baste the raw edge to the lining along the center Front. Top stitch the inner edge to the lining. Cut away each facing to match the shape of the Front neckline.

Sleeve Facings

18 Measure the width of the sleeve pattern 4"–5" above the hem cutting line and add 1". Cut two strips of facing fabric the measured width x 3½"–4" deep. For this jacket, the sleeve facing is pieced with one orphan block and scraps to create the required sleeve width. The depth is determined by the orphan block, so it is almost 5" deep.

19 For this jacket, we didn't have enough lining fabric to cut a full-length sleeve, so the difference is made up with the facing. The sleeve facing was sewn right sides together to the lining with a ¼" seam and then pressed toward the hem to complete the sleeve. Alternatively, the inner edge of the facing can be clean finished, basted, and top stitched to the linings as in step 17.

Stack and Quilt the Jacket Sections

20 Press each fabric layer in preparation for stacking. Assemble the quilt sandwiches for each jacket section: lining right side down, batting, and outer layer right side up. Press the entire sandwich well from both the lining side and the piecing side, beginning in the center and radiating out.

21 Secure the layers together with pins or your preferred method. If desired, use your preferred marking method to mark the stopping points 1" from seam edges. Cut away the batting between the dart legs.

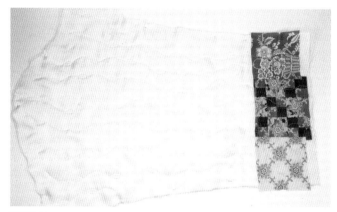

22 Quilt all the way to the edges that will be finished with binding: Center Front, body, sleeve hems, and top of the collar. The quilting was sewn free motion with a darning foot in a simple leaf line pattern, sewing continuously from the top to the bottom of each section.

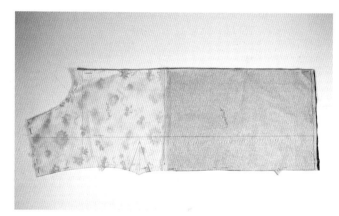

23 Lay the jacket sections back on the cutting table with the corresponding pattern piece. Align the middle horizontal balance line to the sashing on the Front and Back sections. Cut each section to the correct size, trimming away the excess.

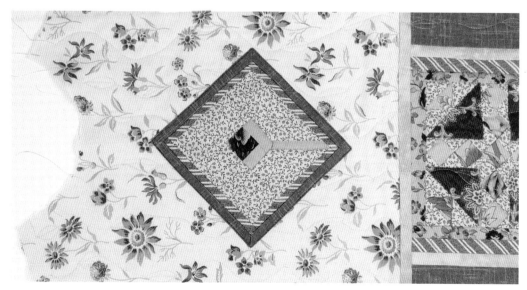

24 Stitch the appliqué block to the Upper Back. For this sample, it was first anchored by stitching-in-the-ditch along a few seam lines within the block, starting from the center and moving outward to avoid creating any "bubbles." Then, the perimeter of the appliqué was edge stitched.

Construct the Jacket Body

This project closely follows the Construct the Opus Jacket or Coat steps 1–6 (page 27) with a few modifications for the quilted-in lining. The seam allowances will be visible inside the jacket and must be finished before moving to the next construction step.

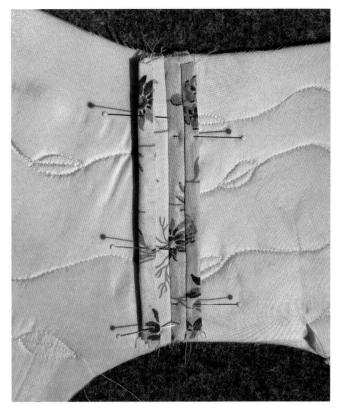

25 Stitch the darts (step 1 of Construct).

26 After sewing the shoulder seams (step 2 of Construct), press the seam allowances open. Carefully trim the batting out of each seam allowance. Cover the raw edge of each seam allowance with a Hong Kong finish (page 35) using strips of the vintage floral fabric.

27 After sewing, clipping, and pressing the underarm seams (step 3 of Construct), measure the length of the underarm seam. Cut and prepare two bias strips 1½" wide x the measured length in yellow fabric. Press in half for the Reversible Seam Binding method (page 37).

28 Machine stitch the binding to the seam allowances, right sides together, along the front of the sleeve. Press binding toward the back of the sleeve, wrapping the raw edge around the seam allowances. Hand stitch the remaining fold of the binding strip to the sleeve lining.

29 If desired, follow directions in the Optional Underarm Sashing sidebar (page 77). Otherwise, after sewing each Sleeve to Side (step 4 of Construct), clip the batting out of the seam allowances. Cover the seam allowances with the Reversible Seam Binding method, as you did for the underarm seams.

Optional Underarm Sashing

For this jacket, a piece of yellow sashing was inserted in the Sleeve-to-Side seam to extend the framing all around the jacket body. Follow these steps to replicate this technique:

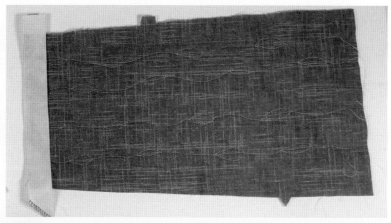

 29a Cut 3/8" away from the top edge of the Side section and the lower edge of the Sleeve, leaving a ¼" seam allowance.

29b Measure the length of this seam and cut two 1" wide sashing strips by the measured length. Sew one strip to the top edge of each Side, right sides together, with a ¼" seam; press strip away from the Side.

29c Cut a binding strip the measured length of the seam x 1¼" wide. Baste this strip to the Sleeve, right side of strip to the lining side of the Sleeve. This will be used to cover the sash seam allowances with a modified Reversible Binding method.

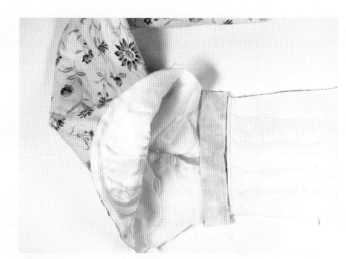

29d Sew the Sleeve to the other raw edge of the sash, right sides together, with a ¼" seam. Press so that the seam allowance fills the sashing.

29e Press the binding strip toward the Side panel, turning the raw edge under. Hand stitch folded edge of binding strip to the Side lining.

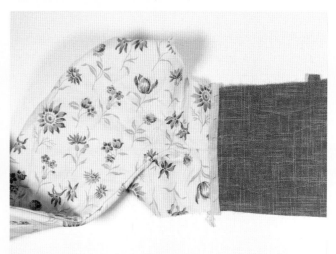

30 After sewing the Side seams (step 5 of Construct), the seam allowances are covered with the Classic Binding Technique (page 38). Take time to fit the jacket (step 6 of Construct) before binding the Side seams:

30a Clip the batting out of all long side seams, removing gathering stitches in the Sleeve head as needed. Trim the seam allowances to ½". Measure one Side seam from the back hem to the front hem and add 2". Prepare two strips of bias binding 2" wide x the calculated length for the Classic Binding Technique.

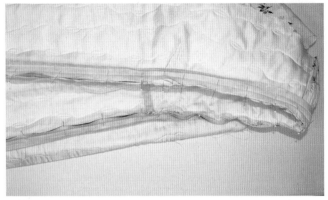

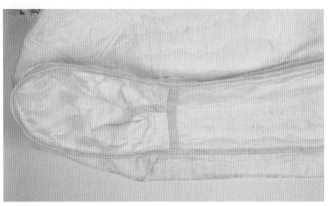

30b Pin one raw edge of the binding to the Side seam, right sides together, on the jacket body side. Stitch the binding to the seam allowance just inside the first fold. Press binding toward the Sleeve/Side unit.

30c Wrap the binding around the seam allowance and pin the loose fold to the seam allowance on the Sleeve/Side unit side. Machine stitch the binding in place just inside the other fold. Press the finished seam allowances toward the Sleeve/Side unit.

Prepare and Insert Collar

31 Prepare ½" wide finished binding from 2" wide bias strips cut from the binding fabric. Approximately 160" (4½ yards) of binding were used to finish the edges of this jacket. Fold and press the binding strips as directed in the Classic Binding Technique.

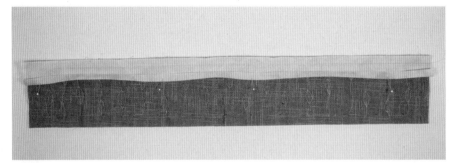

32 Cut two Collars from the fabric and one from batting, remembering to leave an extra ½" on all sides for quilting shrinkage.

33 Stack, press, and secure the layers together. Quilt the Collar, stopping 1" from the edge on the long side that will be attached to the body of the jacket. Recut the quilted Collar to fit the pattern, marking the shoulder dots on the long side. Apply the Classic Binding to the top edge of the collar.

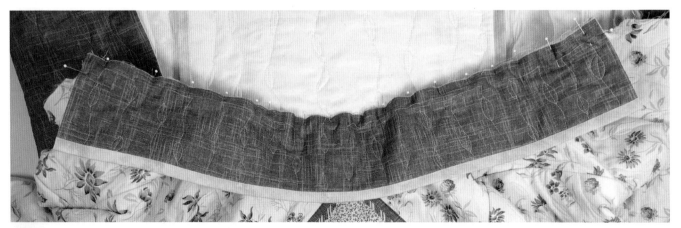

34 Pin the quilted Collar to the neckline with the right side facing up. Ease the Collar into place (step 10 of Construct). Pin generously to incorporate the ease along the ⅝" seam line. Baste the Collar to test the placement. Correct if needed, then sew the seam securely, backstitching at the beginning and end.

35 Trim batting from the seam allowances and clip neckline curves. Trim the seam allowances to ½" and press them toward the Collar.

36 Cut a binding strip 1 ½" wide by the length of the Collar seam from the binding fabric; this strip must be cut on the bias to curve around the neckline. Follow the Reversible Seam Binding Technique to prepare and stitch the binding to the back neck edge at the ⅝" seamline.

37 Press the binding toward the Collar. Wrap and press the final third of the binding to the back of the seam allowances, pressing at each step. Hand stitch the binding to the collar.

Finish the Jacket Edges with Binding   *Use the binding from step 31 in this section.*

Center Fronts

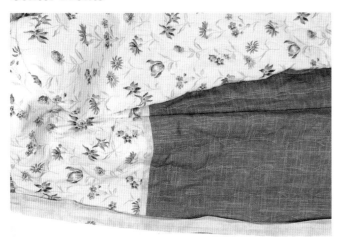

38 Measure the Center Front edges of the jacket from the top of the collar to the hem and add 1". Cut two prepared binding strips the calculated length. Pin the binding, right sides together, to the outer layer of each Center Front, leaving 1" of binding extending beyond the top of the Collar. Stitch along the fold at the ½" seam line, backstitching at each end of the Center Front.

Hem

40 Measure the circumference of the hem and add 2". Cut a prepared binding strip 2" wide by the calculated length. Apply Classic Binding to the hem in the same way as to Center Fronts.

39 Before wrapping the binding to the lining side, open out the bias folds. Press the excess binding at the top of the Collar, wrong sides together, even with the Collar edge. Trim the excess to ½". Refold the binding and wrap it around the edge following the Classic Binding Technique. Press and pin binding to the lining side. Hand stitch in place.

Sleeve Hems

41 Measure the circumference of the sleeve hem and add 1". Cut two prepared binding strips the calculated length. Pin the short ends of each strip, right sides together, to form a circle. Stitch with a ½" seam allowance and press the seam open. Pull the binding loop onto the sleeve hem to make sure it is the correct circumference for each sleeve and adjust if needed.

42 Pin the binding around the sleeve hem, right sides together. Stitch along the fold at ½" to secure the binding. Press binding away from the sleeve.

43 Wrap the binding around the edge following the directions for the Classic Binding Technique to finish each sleeve. Hand stitch to the other side for a smooth bound finish.

Add Buttons and Pockets

44 Lay the selected buttons on the garment to decide how many you want to use and how to place them along Center Front. Practice making buttonholes on the test quilt sandwiches. Make sure the button passes easily through the hole but isn't too loose. Adjust buttonhole size if necessary.

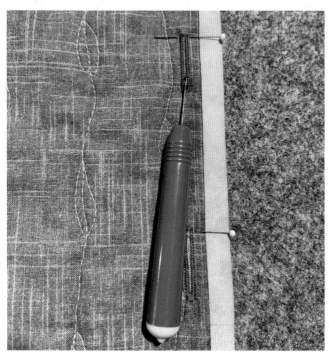

45 Measure the length of the finished buttonhole. Use this measurement to mark the placement on the jacket's Right Front. Draw a line between the points to follow while stitching the buttonholes. After sewing the buttonholes, use a hand sewing needle to bury ½" or so of the thread tails between the quilted layers; snip off the excess.

46 Cut buttonholes open with a buttonhole cutter, seam ripper, or small, sharp scissors. If using a seam ripper or scissors, place a pin through the tack at one end of the buttonhole to ensure you don't rip through the tack while ripping or snipping toward the pin.

47 Pin one pocket on each Front. Stand back to look or take photos to help you determine the best placement, considering distance from the Center Front and from the hem. These pockets straddle the side seams. If desired, stitch-in-the-ditch along the seam line of the last layer of sashing to anchor the pocket.

Tip

The pockets were topstitched to the Fronts at the very end of the project to allow us to make an informed design decision about placement. Whether you choose to topstitch on a seam line or to edge stitch around the perimeter of the pocket, or both, make sure the top corners are secure against the wear and tear of pocket use.

48 Edge stitch around the three sides of the pocket, starting at one upper corner and ending at the other. Strengthen the top corners of each pocket by making a few stitches forward and backward across the top edge of the pocket. A blind stitch or similar presser foot with a metal guide is helpful to maintain straight even stitches; set the needle one or two ticks off the center position so it consistently catches the edge of the block.

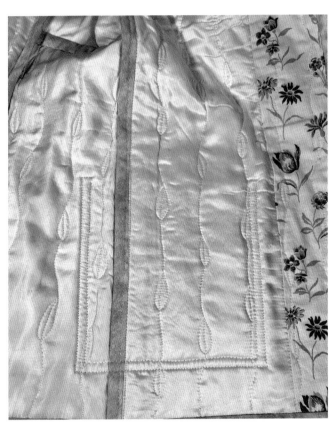

49 At each top corner of a pocket, pull the thread tails to the lining side, tie a knot, and bury ½"–1" of the tails between the quilted layers with a hand needle. Snip off the remainder.

50 Lay the jacket on a table with Center Fronts overlapped by 2". Use a pin to mark the location of each button opening on the left front of the jacket. Sew each button near the top of the buttonhole.

Reversible Collage Coat

Size Pictured: Adult XL

Designing a reversible coat, especially one with such disparate sides, requires thought and planning once a group of fabrics is assembled. For this coat, it was important that the two colorways appear coordinated in the shoulder and collar area because elements of each side are visible from the reverse side. This was accomplished by adding a small yoke to the back and fronts of the reverse side using medium-colored prints that coordinate with the binding fabrics. Softly lilting free motion quilting anchors the many appliqués in the collage.

When planning a collage project, the design process and pattern manipulation are effectively done in tandem. Double the challenge with a reversible coat like this one!

Note: For this project, the light-colored collage side is referred to as the primary side. The darker print side is referred to as the reverse side.

MATERIALS NEEDED

- 2 Opus patterns, shirt collar style, coat length, roll back cuff

- 1½–2 yards of light-colored cotton for Sleeves and middle landscape of primary side

- 1–1½ yards of darker coordinating cotton for lower landscape of primary side

- 1 yard of sky-like coordinating cotton for the upper landscape and Collars of primary side

- (2) 43" x 24" panels or 2 coordinating panels (we used Imperial Collection 18 Camellia Panel from Robert Kaufman) for cutting collage elements and Sleeve cuffs

- 1–1¾ yards of dark cotton print for body of lining layer

- 2–2½ yards of dark cotton for Sleeves and Sides of lining layer

- ½ yard dark cotton for Sleeve and Side bindings of lining layer

- 1½ yards of medium-colored cotton for bindings, Collar, and yoke of lining layer

- Batting, as needed for the selected size (we used Hobbs Tuscany Silk)

- Thread (we used Aurifil 40 wt.) for collage, quilting, and construction

- 5 sets of gold decorative snaps

Design Features

- **The coat is completely reversible.**

- **Fabric is stacked on the Fronts and Backs of the primary side.**

- **Raw-edge collage cut from a fabric panel decorates the Fronts and Back of the primary side.**

- **All seams are covered using the Reversible Seam Binding Technique.**

- **Snap closures are used as a finish.**

Design and Prepare the Patterns

1 Plan the landscape and collage elements of the primary side on one set of Front and full Back patterns. Lay down the three elements of the landscape first, drawing them right onto the pattern.

2 Create patterns for each of the three elements of the primary side landscape. Where the pattern has been divided, add a seam allowance to each cut edge. If desired, create a back yoke pattern the same way for the reverse side pattern. In this sample jacket, the primary side yoke and reverse side yoke have different shapes and cut lines.

3 Use the border print for the roll back cuff. Create a cuff pattern, or simply calculate the cuff measurement, both width and length. Draw a seam line for the cuff and on the Sleeve pattern, then add a cutting line ⅝" below to indicate the length to be cut to accommodate the cuff. Shorten the Sleeve pattern before cutting out the reverse-side Sleeves: draw a seam line for the cuff on the pattern; draw a cutting line ⅝" below the seam line; and fold the paper below the new cutting line out of the way.

Prepare the Layers

4 Cut out the three landscape elements in the selected fabrics for each primary Front and Back. Remember to add ½" on each perimeter edge to accommodate possible quilting uptake. Press under the added seam allowance for the upper and lower landscape.

5 Lay the landscape elements on the Front and Back primary patterns, positioning the middle first, then placing the upper and lower landscape. Pin them together to retain the size needed when the quilt sandwiches are stacked.

6 Cut out the collage elements from the panel, leaving a bit of fabric around the outside edges. Place the elements to create a pleasing picture. Take time to walk away and revisit the composition; rearrange if the design seems imperfect. Read Tips for Successful Free Motion Stitching with Raw-Edge Collage (page 87) for more directions.

7 Cut two Sleeves and two Sides for the primary side using the chosen fabrics, remembering to add ½" all around the perimeter edges for quilting uptake.

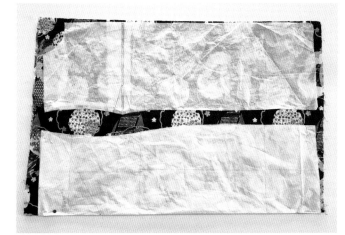

8 Cut out the Yoke and Lower Fronts and Back for the reverse side from the chosen fabric, remembering to add ½" all around the perimeter edges for quilting uptake.

9 Cut two shortened Sleeves from the designated fabric for the reverse side, remembering to add ½" all around the perimeter edges for quilting uptake. Cut two cuffs as calculated with the cuff pattern. Cut two Sides for the reverse-side primary layer. Cut out a Collar for the primary side and a Collar for the reverse side.

10 Unfold the pattern pieces to their full size and cut out one layer of batting for each coat section, adding ½" all around each pattern to accommodate quilting uptake. Cut away the batting from between the dart legs.

Collage and Quilt the Sections

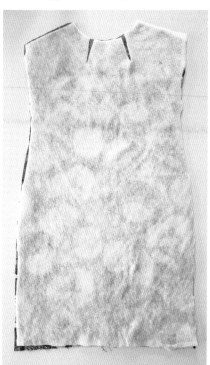

11 Assemble the Back and Fronts of the reverse side by pinning the Yokes, right sides together, to the corresponding Lower Fronts and Back. Stitch them together using a ⅝" seam and press the seams open.

12 Assemble the reverse-side Sleeves by pinning the cuffs to the Sleeves, right sides together. Stitch them together using a ⅝" seam and press the seams open.

13 Lay the reverse-layer Front and Back pieces face down on a table. Add the batting on top of the reverse-side pieces. Press these two layers together well.

14 Lay the primary-layer landscape pieces for the Front and Back sections on top of the batting and press flat. Lay the elements of the collage on top of the landscape pieces and press well.

Reversible Collage Coat   **85**

15 Once the collage design is finalized, pin all the elements of the composition in place using small dressmaker pins. Even if you choose to use a temporary adhesive spray to hold the collage elements in place, a few pins are usually needed.

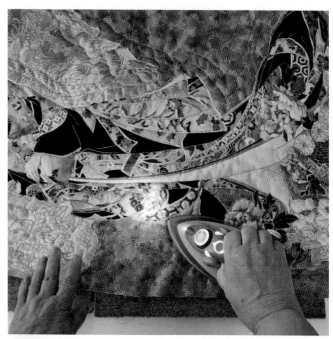

16 Begin quilting the collage in the center of the composition. All the edges of each appliqué should be anchored in the free motion quilting process. Plan for quilting in the interior of large appliqués. Whenever you stop stitching and before beginning to stitch again, press the piece from both the primary side and the reverse side to make sure it looks presentable on both sides.

17 Use free motion echo quilting or another simple technique to quilt the remaining areas of each section. Remember to leave a 1" unquilted area around the perimeter edges of each section. Press well.

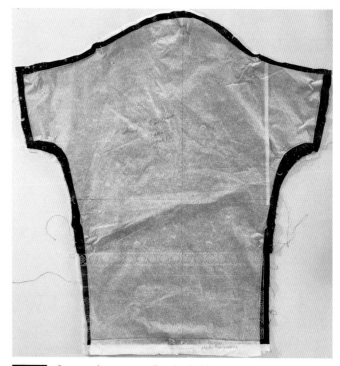

18 Stack the three layers of each Sleeve, each Side, and the Collar together. Place the reverse side face down, batting in the middle, and finally the primary layer face up. Press well and pin the layers together smoothly. Quilt each of these sections using a free motion pattern like the one used in the uncollaged areas of the Fronts and Back. Remember to leave 1" unquilted around the perimeter edges of each section,

19 Press each section well on both the primary side and the reverse side. Place the pattern piece on top of each corresponding section, matching the pattern to the darts first. Pin the pattern in place and cut each section to the correct size, trimming away any fabric that extends beyond the pattern.

Tips for Successful Free Motion Stitching with Raw-Edge Collage

Use these tips to ensure your free motion collage composition is a success:

- Make an elaborate sample to test stitching, ways to stitch different elements, etc.

- When you are cutting each raw-edge appliqué out, leave a small bit of background fabric (⅛" at most) to make the stitching easier. It can be trimmed away later.

- Use small dressmaker pins with tiny heads to hold the pressed collage pieces in place. These can glide right under the free motion quilting foot to keep everything stable. Spray adhesive may also be used but can make the fabric stiff and gum up the needle. Use sparingly if desired.

- Quilt as desired to anchor each piece of fabric in the collage.

- Keep 1" unquilted all around the perimeter of each section. After the coat is assembled, additional quilting can be added.

- Press regularly on both sides.

- Keep the quilting style around the collaged appliqués simple, like an echo of the collage motif.

- Take regular breaks from stitching; assess and press the piece when you take a break.

- Every time you change the bobbin, do a little test stitching on the sample to make sure the tension is correct.

Special tips for reversible coats with one side that has collage:

- Choose fabric with a busy pattern for the reverse side so the quilting that follows the collage design is not a distraction.

- Use scrap fabrics to make samples.

- Choose a thread for each side that matches well.

- Pay careful attention to the tension of the two threads, stitch quality, and color on each side.

- Stop and press from both sides occasionally if the collage is large.

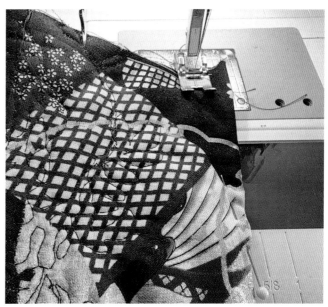

20 Sew the darts (step 1 of Construct the Opus Jacket or Coat, page 27). Press well and topstitch the lower edge of the dart to the coat to ensure neat darts on each side of the reversible coat. Be sure the thread in both the needle and the bobbin are correct for sewing on the two layers.

21 Pin the Fronts to the Back at the shoulders, primary sides together (step 2 of Construct). Stitch the shoulder seams with the reverse side facing up. Press the seam allowances toward the Back, trim batting out of the seam allowances, and grade the seams down to no more than ½".

22 Cut two bias binding strips, 1½" wide x the length of the shoulder seam. Press in thirds as described in Reversible Seam Binding (page 37).

23 Pin one raw edge of the binding to the front side of each shoulder seam, aligning the fold with the shoulder seam. Stitch just inside the fold. Press the binding toward the seam. Wrap the binding around the seam allowance, pin in place along the back shoulder, and hand stitch it neatly in place; press well.

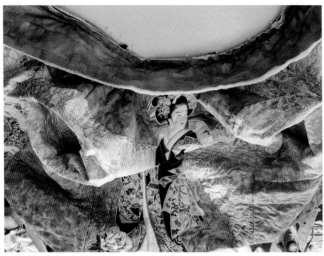

24 Pin the quilted Collar to the coat neckline with the primary layer facing up and the reverse layer against the coat. Ease the Collar into place (step 10 of Construct). Pin generously to incorporate the ease along the ⅝" seam line. Sew the seam securely, backstitching at the beginning and end. Press the seam allowances toward the Collar, trim batting out of the seam allowances, and grade the seams down to no more than ½".

25 Cut a bias-binding strip to the length of the collar seam x 1½" width. Apply the binding on the Collar seam with Reversible Seam Binding. Clip the seam allowances generously before wrapping them with the binding so the Collar will lay flat. Press well at each step, and hand stitch the binding to the Collar.

26 Pin and then stitch the underarm seam of each Sleeve, primary sides together (step 3 of Construct). Press the seam allowances toward the back, trim batting out of the seam allowances, and grade the seams down to no more than ½". Clip the curve in the seam well.

27 Cut two bias binding strips 1½" wide x the measured length of the Sleeve seam. Attach the binding to the front side of the seam, then wrap the remaining binding around the seam, press, pin, and hand stitch in place with Reversible Seam Binding.

28 Sew each Sleeve to the corresponding Side, primary sides together (step 4 of Construct). Press the seam allowances toward the Side, trim batting out of the seam allowances, and grade the seams down to no more than ½".

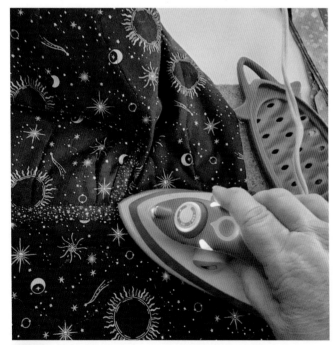

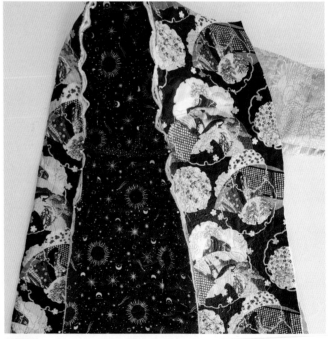

29 Measure and cut bias binding strips for Reversible Seam Binding, 1½" wide x the length of the seam. Attach each binding strip to the Sleeve side of the seam, wrap, and finish the binding with hand stitches

30 Insert the Sleeve/Sides into the Front/Back (step 5 of Construct). Take a minute to try on the coat and make any necessary fitting adjustments before continuing. Press the seam allowances toward the Sleeve/Side, trim batting out of the seam allowances, and grade the seams down to no more than ½".

31 Prepare two bias Reversible Seam Bindings 1½" wide x the length of one long Side seam (measured from front hem to back hem). Piece this binding strip if necessary. Carefully pin one unfolded edge of the binding all around the Front/Back side of the seam. Be sure there is no slack as you pin, especially around the sleeve cap, and then stitch the binding in place. Press the binding toward the Side/Sleeve, wrap, pin in place, and finish the binding with hand stitches. Work slowly around the Sleeve heads, which are tricky. Press well after removing the pins.

Finish the Edges and Add Closures

32 Give the coat a good press all over. This coat required 4½ yards of joining strips and ½" double fold Classic Binding (page 38). Cut it all at once and prepare by pressing in the folds as directed in the Classic Binding Technique.

33 Finish each raw edge of the Collar, coat hem, Sleeve hems, and Center Fronts (step 12 of Construct). When a second binding crosses an already-attached binding, an extra 1" needs to be added to the length to finish the ends. Join some strips of binding for the long hem edge. If possible, avoid piecing the binding up the Fronts of the coat.

34 Because the coat is reversible, be sure to apply the binding, right sides together, to the primary side at each step. Then wrap the binding around to the reverse side for finishing. However, be sure to hand stitch it with extra care on the reverse side as it will also be seen!

35 Determine the desired location of the snap closures, measure, and mark them with pins or chalk. Hand stitch them onto the coat so they align perfectly. Because there is a 2" overlap in the front of the coat, plan to locate the snaps ½" inside the binding edge.

Repurposed Quilt Duster

Size Pictured: Adult Small

A fully finished quilt can be repurposed to create a striking quilted coat. There is a great deal of variability in a repurposing project because of the infinite variety of quilts—differing in size, color, design, and so on. Every repurposed quilt coat will be entirely unique!

The duster length means the hem extends 9" longer than the coat-length pattern. The existing quilt bindings are incorporated into the coat as the finishing edges along the Center Front, hems, and collar. The finished duster includes in-seam pockets and back vents to allow ease of movement. Most seam allowances are clean finished with overcast stitches on a serger; a few others are covered with a Hong Kong finish. Hand worked thread loops are applied along the right Center Front for the extra-large buttons.

MATERIALS NEEDED

- Opus pattern, shirt collar style, coat length
- Twin-size or larger quilt (we used 58" x 72"), cleaned and repaired as needed
- ½–1 yard fabric (we used a cotton batik similar to original binding) for binding and pocket linings
- Thread (we used Gutermann Mara 100) for construction and finishing
- Button hole thread for loops
- 3 buttons about 1¾" wide

Design Features

- Repurposes a finished quilt.
- Extends the pattern length for duster-style coat.
- Vents are added at the hemline in back side seams.
- In-seam pockets inserted in front side seams (optional).
- Hand-worked thread loops for large buttons.

Prepare the Quilt

Inspect the quilt you have selected. This duster was made with a quilt that only needed washing. In many cases, you will be working with an older quilt that may be worn, damaged, discolored, stained, or dirty. If so, do a rough layout of the pattern on the quilt to determine which areas need to be repaired and whether you will be able to work around the most damaged or stained areas.

Repair tears before washing the quilt. Badly damaged elements can be covered by stitching fabric scraps in a similar color or mood, or from unused sections of the quilt, over the damaged areas. Cut the scrap to the shape of the damaged piece with an extra ¼" around the edges. Turn the raw edges under, and hand stitch the patch over the damaged piece with invisible stitches. Add quilting stitches over the top that mimic the quilt's style if desired to blend in better.

To remove stains or other discoloration, soak the quilt for several hours in a solution of nonchlorine bleach or enzyme cleaner dissolved into water. Machine wash on gentle cycle in cool water then lay flat to dry, in the sun if possible.

Prepare the Patterns

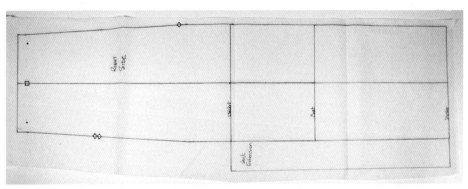

1 Trace a full set of patterns onto tissue paper. Lengthen the Back, Fronts, and Sides by 9", or to your preferred length, to extend the cutting lines at the Side seams, Center Front, and grainlines; add paper if necessary. Use a ruler to draw the new duster-length cutting line parallel to the coat-length cutting line.

2 Add a vent extension to the Side patterns to cover the vent opening. On the Right and Left Side patterns, add a 2" wide rectangle along the back Side seam (the side with double notches) extending from the jacket cutting line to the new duster cutting line.

3 If adding optional in-seam pockets, cut out or trace two pocket patterns with the notches and dot markings.

4 Make sure you have traced the horizontal balance lines, grainlines, hem lines, dots, and notches onto every pattern piece. Label each piece with the name of the pattern piece, Right or Left, etc.

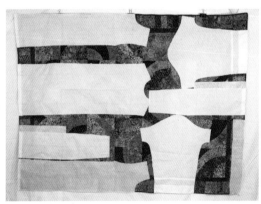

6 Cut all coat sections out of the quilt. Cut the pattern exactly, including notches and other markings, because an extra ½" is not needed for quilting. Cut four pocket pieces: two from quilt scraps and two from binding fabric or other stash fabric.

5 Use the full set of pattern pieces to lay out the entire coat before cutting. Try several different layouts; consider which elements of the quilt to feature on the Front and Back or avoid. Lay the primary pattern pieces on the quilt elements you most want to feature first, then fit the others around them in a logical way. Take a photo or draw a sketch of a layout you may want to come back to before moving the pieces around again.

Bind Vent Extension

7 Measure the length of the vent extension added onto the Side patterns and add 4"–5". Prepare two 2" wide strips x the calculated length, using the Classic Binding method (page 38).

8 Open a pressed binding and pin it, right sides together, to one vent extension, letting 1" of binding extend beyond the hem. Starting at the hem, sew binding along the fold, stopping ½" from the corner. Remove the Side from the machine.

My Quilt Isn't Big Enough!

If you cannot fit all pattern pieces on the quilt, consider these options:

- If just a wee bit more is needed, try shortening the coat's length. For example, 10" was originally added to the length of the Front, Back, and Side patterns for this coat. During layout, they were each shortened by 1" to be able to fit all sections on the quilt.

- Cut the coat from two (or more) quilts that work well together.

- The Side panels, Sleeves, or Collar may be cut out of a coordinating fabric. Those sections would each need to be quilted to a batting and inner layer. Choose materials that will be comparable to the quilt in weight and flexibility, and use a quilting style and thread that blends with the original quilt.

- Divide some of the pattern pieces to provide more flexibility in the layout. For example, the Back or Fronts could be divided into an upper yoke and lower portion. Some of the pieces could then be cut from coordinating fabric, or they might all fit on the quilt more easily.

9 To turn the corner, fold binding up and away from the vent at a 45-degree angle; pin in place temporarily. Fold binding back down, making the fold even with the raw edge of the vent, and pin in place along the short edge of the vent extension.

10 Return to the machine to stitch along the top edge, stopping at the corner where the extension meets the side. Cut off excess binding to ½". Fold the remainder to the wrong side of the binding and press for a clean finish.

Repurposed Quilt Duster   **93**

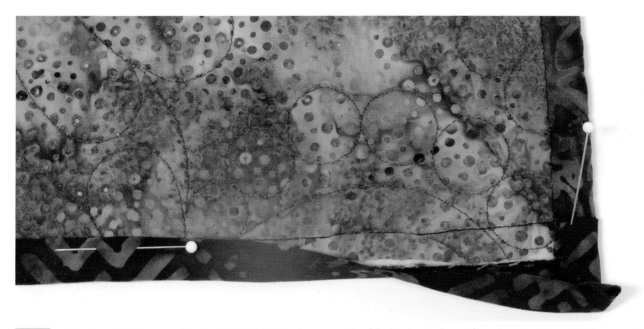

11 At the hem, trim the excess binding to ½." Fold it into the wrong side of the binding and press for a clean finish. Press binding away from the extension, then wrap it around to the wrong side of the vent extension to encase the raw edge, pinning in place. Hand or machine stitch the binding to the wrong side of coat along vent extension.

Attach Pockets to Fronts and Sides

If not adding the optional pockets to your project, skip to the next section, Construct the Coat.

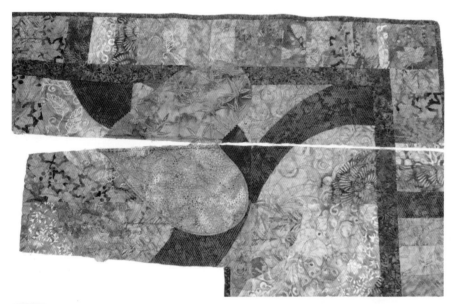

12 Clean finish the rounded raw edge of each quilted pocket. Pin a quilted pocket to each Side, right sides together, matching at the notches. The notches place the pockets just above the Opus jacket hem, but they may be moved up or down to better fit the wearer's height and arm length. Pin a fabric pocket to each Front, right sides together, matching at the notches. Sew pockets to Sides and Fronts with a ¼" seam allowance.

13 Press the pockets away from the Sides and Fronts. Clean finish the raw edge of the pocket seams with overlock stitching if desired.

Construct the Coat

14 Stitch the darts (step 1 of Construct the Opus Jacket or Coat, page 27).

15 After sewing the shoulder seams (step 2 of Construct), press the seam allowances open. Cover the raw edge of each seam allowance with a Hong Kong finish (page 35).

16 After sewing the underarm seam on each sleeve (step 3 of Construct), clip the underarm curve and press the seam allowances open. Separately overlock stitch the raw edge of each seam allowance.

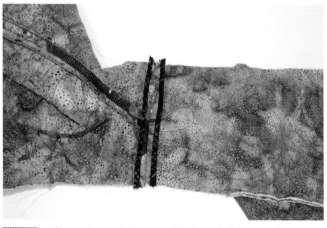

17 After sewing each Sleeve to Side (step 4 of Construct), press the seam allowances open. Cover each raw edge with a Hong Kong finish or clean finish with overlock stitching.

18 At Construct step 5, pin the pocket to the pocket lining right sides together along the rounded edges while pinning each Front to Side. Sew the pocket as part of the side seam, leaving an opening between the dots indicated on the pocket pattern. Backstitch securely at each end of the pocket opening.

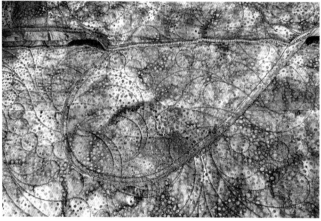

19 While sewing the back Side seam (step 5 of Construct), stop stitching about 1" below the pattern's jacket cutting line and backstitch securely. Press the seam allowances open and finish the raw edges of the Side seams with overlock stitches, ending at the jacket cutting line in back. In the Sleeve head, press both seam allowances toward the Sleeve for support.

20 Press and pin the pockets toward the Fronts. Hand stitch the outer edge of each finished pocket to the inside of the coat's Fronts, burying the stitches between the quilted layers.

Prepare and Insert the Collar

21 For this coat, two of the three Collar edges were already finished with the original quilt binding. A piece of the original quilt binding was removed from a quilt scrap and reapplied to finish the third edge. If the Collar is not already bound, follow the directions for the Classic Binding Technique to bind the top and short sides of the Collar.

22 Insert the collar into the duster (step 10 of Construct). After trimming and clipping the seam allowances, bind the neckline seam with Reversible Seam Binding (page 37). If possible, release quilting stitches in the neckline seam allowances and trim away the batting to reduce bulk.

Finish the Vent

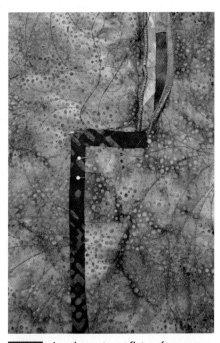

23 Finish the vent opening along the Back seam with a Hong Kong finish, folding the short ends of the binding strip inside the binding for a clean finish at the top of the vent opening and at the hem.

24 Firmly press the finished seam allowance toward the wrong side of the coat. Hand stitch along the Hong Kong finished edge to secure this seam allowance in place.

25 Lay the coat on a flat surface wrong side up, allowing the vent extension to overlap the Back. Pin the upper 2" of the extension closed. Hand stitch the upper 2" of the extension's bound edge to the inside of the coat, burying the stitches between the quilted layers.

26 From the right side of the coat, topstitch the upper 2" of the vent extension. To make this stitching less noticeable, stitch on top of the existing quilting stitches. It can also be topstitched with an X or an upside-down V across the 2" square.

Add Buttons and Loops

27 Plan the placement of the buttons and button loops. Mark the top and bottom of each loop, approximately the width of the button.

28 Thread a needle with quilting or buttonhole thread approximately 36" long, doubled and knotted neatly. Bring the needle into the wrong side at the binding, allowing the knot to anchor between the coat and the binding. Push the needle through the binding and out the crease.

29 Create a series of loops anchored at each end of the button markings. It should be slightly curved away from the binding. Stitch a knot at each end of each new loop after checking that all threads are an even length. Test the opening to see if the button can slide through and adjust if necessary.

30 Once you have at least eight loops (four passes with thread doubled), make another knot. Bury the remaining thread in the lining and clip.

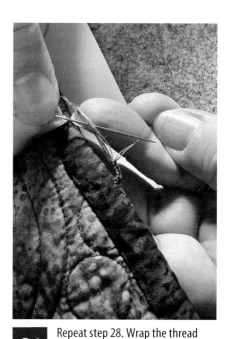

31 Repeat step 28. Wrap the thread loops with the buttonhole stitch for extra stability, adjusting the thread for a smooth application after each stitch. When you reach the other side of the large loop, anchor the thread in the binding with a knot and bury the thread tails in the wrong side.

32 Attach the buttons on the quilted duster. These jumbo buttons are supported with a small plastic button on the back side to prevent tearing a hole in the cloth from wear and tear with the buttons.

Wholecloth and Collage Jacket

Size Pictured: Kids 8

In this project, each wholecloth outer section is decorated with small appliqués for pops of colorful interest. The appliqués are placed on each outer section before the layers are stacked into the quilt sandwich. The appliqués are permanently attached when the sections are quilted with a free motion technique known as stippling. Like the Assorted Patchwork Jacket (page 60), this jacket features a narrow front band and roll back cuff.

MATERIALS NEEDED

- Opus pattern, front band style, jacket length, extend sleeve pattern 2" for roll back cuff

- 1½–2 yards of quilting cotton for outer layer

- 1½–2 yards of quilting cotton for lining and ties

- Batting, as needed for the selected size (we used Hobbs Thermore® Batting)

- ¼ yard of cotton print for the Band and Sleeve finishes

- 75 small, raw-edge, square and rectangle appliqués

- Water-soluble, double-sided fusible tape (we used Dritz Wash Away Wonder Tape)

- Thread (we used Sulky 30 wt. Cotton) for quilting

- Thread (we used Gutermann TERA 80) for construction

Design Features

- Small, raw-edge appliqués are added to the Back, Fronts, Sleeves, and Sides before quilting.

- Uses a quilted-in lining; though the Sleeve lining was pieced because there was not enough lining fabric.

- Each section of the jacket is free motion quilted with stippling.

- Coordinating ties work as this jacket's closures.

Create the Fabric

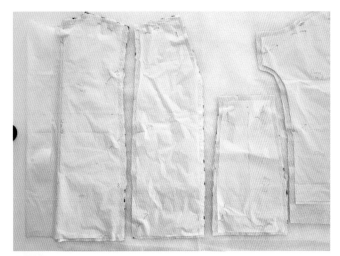

1 Using the prepared pattern, cut out the Back, Fronts, Sleeves, and Sides from the outer layer fabric, batting, and lining. Remember to cut each section an additional ½" larger on all sides to accommodate shrinkage after quilting.

2 Arrange the appliqués on each piece of the outer layer, being mindful of how each section looks next to its neighboring sections. For successful free motion quilting, attach each individual appliqué with fusible tape; these were secured with ¼" wide tape cut to fit each side of the appliqué.

3 Press each fabric layer in preparation for stacking. Assemble the quilt sandwiches for each jacket section with the lining right side down, batting in the center, and prepared outer fabric right side facing up. Once the three layers are stacked, press the entire sandwich well, beginning in the center and radiating out from both the lining side and the piecing side.

4 Secure the layers together with pins or your preferred method in preparation for quilting.

Quilting the Sections

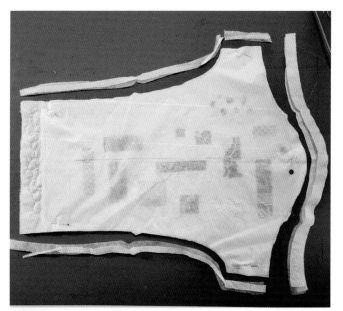

5 Free motion quilt each section, keeping 1" all around each section unquilted. This jacket is quilted with a bubble design. Quilt with the outer layer facing up so the appliqués can be anchored smoothly in the free motion stitching. If there are threads associated with the starts and stops of the free motion quilting, tie them off on the lining side and bury the threads in the quilted layers.

6 Once each section is quilted and pressed, lay the pattern piece on the section and trim away any excess fabric around the edges. Don't forget to cut or mark the single and double notches on each section for easy construction.

Construct the Jacket

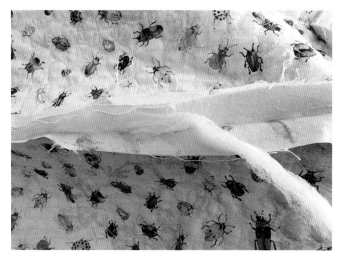

7 Assemble the jacket following Construct the Opus Jacket or Coat steps 1–7 (page 27). To reduce the bulk within the seam allowances, carefully trim away the batting outside the seam lines. Press the seam allowances after the batting is cut away and before clean finishing each seam.

Tip

If possible, try the jacket on the wearer and check the fit at Construct step 6 before trimming the batting from the side seam allowances. Make any fitting changes before moving forward.

Not Enough Fabric for Cutting and Piecing?

In our sample, there was not enough of the bug-motif lining fabric but plenty of the white-on-white outer fabric. To make things work, the top of the Sleeve was cut in the extra outer fabric and the bottom of the Sleeve was cut in the print to accommodate a roll back cuff. The fabric was stitched together in advance of stacking and quilting the Sleeve sandwiches.

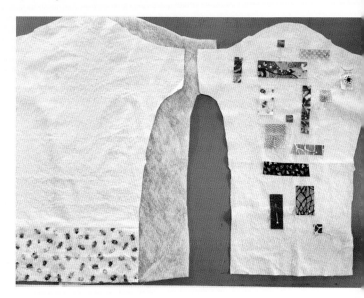

8 Clean finish the exposed seam allowances for durability and a pleasing appearance. This jacket's seams and hem edge were finished with a three-thread overlock on a serger, but a zigzag or overlock stitch on a sewing machine will also work. If you prefer hand finishes, an overcast or blanket stitch will be beautiful too.

9 After finishing and pressing the side seams toward the Sleeve/Side unit, hem the jacket body with a turned-up hem (step 7 of Construct).

Wholecloth and Collage Jacket **101**

Add Binding to Sleeve Hems

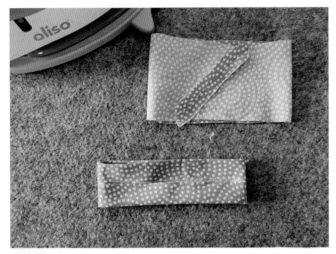

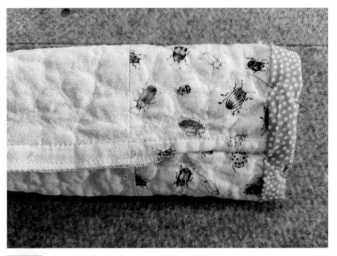

10 Measure the circumference of the Sleeve hem and add 1". Cut two bias strips the calculated length by 2" wide. Cutting the binding so the seams are on the straight of grain is ideal to distribute the seam bulk in the lining. Stitch each binding into a circle with a ½" seam allowance and press the seam open.

11 Use Classic Binding (page 38) to finish each Sleeve. Be mindful that kids' jackets have very small Sleeve circumferences, so stitch on the machine carefully and use hand stitches for a smooth bound finish. Fold under the clean-finished Sleeve seam edge for a neater cuff before hand stitching the binding.

Narrow Center Front Band and Ties

12 Measure the jacket from center back to hem, and calculate length needed for the front Band (step 9 of Construct). Cut two rectangles 2¾" wide x the calculated length. This will create a narrow ¾" wide finished Band. Narrow Bands can be cut on the straight grain or on the bias. Stitch the Band pieces together along one short side and press open the center back seam.

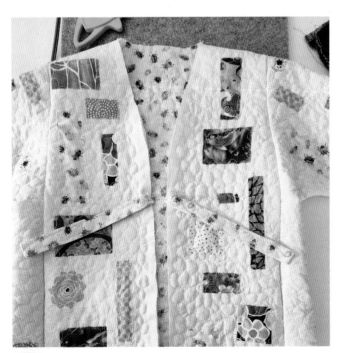

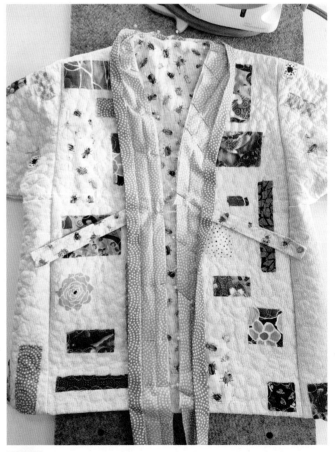

13 Create the ties for the jacket closure by following the steps in the sidebar (page 103). Attach a tie to each Front in the chest area.

14 Attach the Band as you would a front Band (step 9 of Construct) but do not interface. Finish the narrow Band with the Classic Binding technique, hand stitching the last step.

Create Front Tie Closures

The ties on the Wholecloth and Collage Jacket are 7" x ¾" when finished. They are filled with one layer of batting to add loft and keep them neat. Interfacing could be used instead of batting to support the ties.

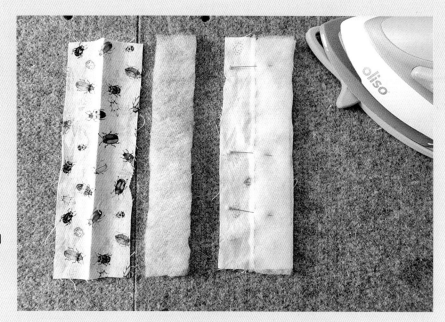

13a Cut two 8" x 2½" strips of fabric and two 8" x 1½" pieces of batting. Fold the fabric in half lengthwise and press. Open and place right side down. Pin batting to one side of the fabric.

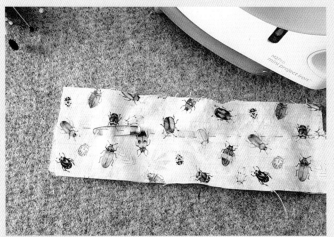
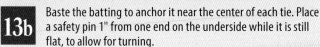

13b Baste the batting to anchor it near the center of each tie. Place a safety pin 1" from one end on the underside while it is still flat, to allow for turning.

13c Stitch the tie with a ½" seam down the long edge and along the short edge where the pin was placed.

13d Trim away the batting in the seam allowance, then grade and clip the seam allowances. Turn each tie by pulling the safety pin through the open end of the tie.

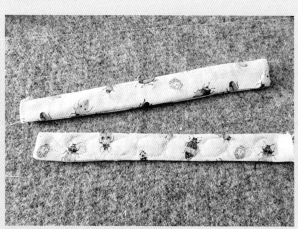

13e Press well and quilt or topstitch as desired to match the quilting in the jacket.

Orphan Blocks Front Band Jacket

Size Pictured: Kids 10

Many quilters and sewists have unfinished projects and leftover "orphan" blocks in their stash. This jacket was designed around a collection of orphan blocks, which we hope will inspire you to dive into your own stash for resource materials and see how to incorporate them into your own quilted jackets.

The 10 orphan blocks encircle the jacket's hem, and they feature in a back yoke and at the sleeve hems. The blocks are pieced together with a collection of scrap fabric, the author's stash, and vintage fabrics. The polyester lining also includes a cotton yoke for support and a pleated back. Closure is provided by three buttons and buttonholes.

MATERIALS NEEDED

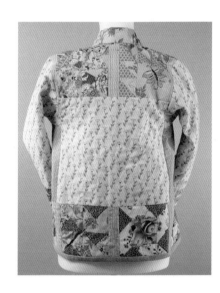

- Opus pattern, front band style, jacket length
- (10) 6" x 6" quilt blocks
- 1–2 yards coordinating cotton prints for Fronts, Back, and Sleeves
- ½–¾ yard of coordinating fabric for the Sides and hem binding
- Scrap fabric for the front Band, yokes, and sashing
- 1½–2½ yards of silky fabric (we used polyester) for lining
- Vintage shirting scraps for sashing
- Cotton scraps for lining's yoke, optional
- Batting, as needed for the selected size (we used Quilters Dream Bamboo)
- Thread (we used Wonderfil Tutti™, variegated) for quilting
- Thread (we used Gutermann Mara 100) for construction
- 3 buttons

Design Features

- Orphan quilt blocks are joined with sashes to create a pieced hemline, cuff decoration, and back yoke.
- Vintage and modern fabrics connect colors that were challenging to match.
- Spray starch gives body to the lightweight vintage shirting.
- The free-hanging lining has a cotton yoke to add support to the shoulder area.

Design and Pattern Work

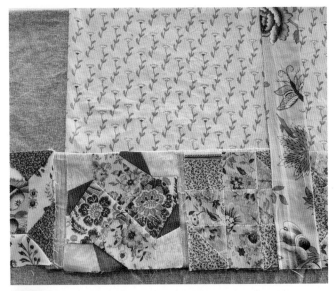

1 Plan the jacket design based on the number of blocks available, their size, and the garment size you are making. For further inspiration, read sidebar Mixing Vintage and Modern Fabrics (page 70). The orphan blocks will be used all the way around the hemline, on the upper back, and for the sleeve cuffs.

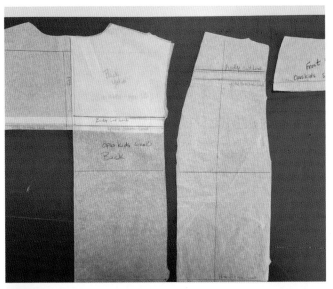

2 Working with the Front pattern, cut a yoke from scrap fabric and draw a seam line. Trace a separate Front Yoke pattern piece onto tissue paper, and add a ⅝" seam allowance below the seam line. On the Front pattern, add a ⅝" seam allowance above the seam line; fold the pattern back above this line.

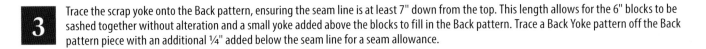

3 Trace the scrap yoke onto the Back pattern, ensuring the seam line is at least 7" down from the top. This length allows for the 6" blocks to be sashed together without alteration and a small yoke added above the blocks to fill in the Back pattern. Trace a Back Yoke pattern off the Back pattern piece with an additional ¼" added below the seam line for a seam allowance.

4 Arrange the orphan blocks along the lower edge of the Front, Back, and Side pattern pieces for the hem. Calculate the width of the sashes needed to complete each lower pattern edge with the planned blocks and sashes; for our sample, we needed 1½" wide strips to result in 1" wide finished sashes.

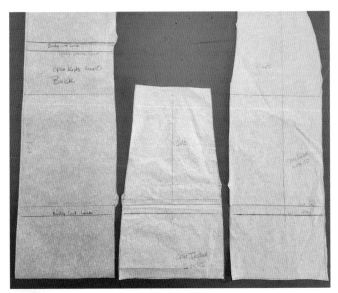

5 Alter the Front, Back, and Side pattern pieces to reflect the hem blocks. Draw a seam line 6" up from the hemline and then a ⅝" seam allowance below that.

Note on Patterns

The full Front, Back, and Side pattern pieces are needed to cut the batting and lining and to trim the quilted sections. Because they are being split into sections for the outer layer, we simply folded each pattern back along the identified cutting lines when cutting out the shortened mid-sections. Similarly, the Sleeve pieces were altered to accommodate their 6" hem additions. If you prefer, trace and cut out separate pattern pieces for each hemline block, Yoke, and mid-section, but keep your original pattern pieces intact.

Cut and Construct the Outer Layer

6 Cut out the Front, Back, and Sleeve mid-sections from chosen fabric using the altered patterns. Remember to add an extra ½" on all perimeter edges for quilting uptake. Cut the altered Sides from the coordinating fabric using the same method.

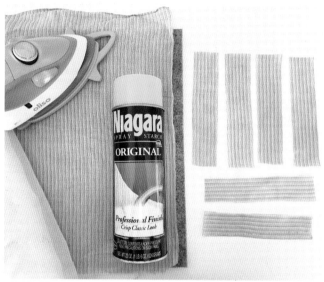

7 Spray starch very lightweight fabrics, like this vintage shirting, before cutting the 1½" x 6" sashing strips. This helps in cutting the fabric sashes successfully.

8 For each Front and Side hem section, stitch each orphan block together with two sashing strips using ¼" seams. For the Back hem, combine two blocks with one sash and then add sashing strips on the outer edge of each block. Press well.

9 Stitch the Front, Back, and Side hem sections to their respective mid-sections, right sides together. Add a ⅝" seam allowance to the fabric middles, but use your judgment as to how much seam allowance will be used on the pieced sections. Here, a ¼" seam was used on the pieced sections.

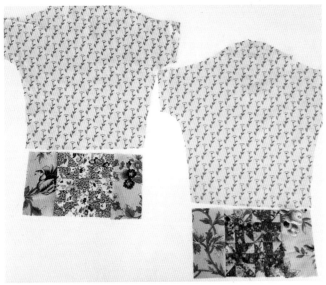

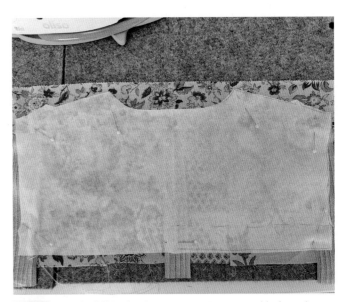

10 Using the Sleeve pattern as a guide, cut sashing strips to anchor the block positioned at the hem of each Sleeve. For this sample, fabric scraps were used to create the lower edge of each Sleeve.

11 Use the full Back Yoke pattern to arrange two blocks and three sashing strips. Cut additional fabric at the top. Use the same fabric at the top of the Back Yoke to cut the Front Yokes. Use a ¼" seam to join all the pieces for the Back Yoke. Cut based on the pattern, leaving ½" around the perimeter.

12 Stitch each Yoke, right sides together, to the top of the Front and Back section respectively. Press the seam allowances down toward the mid-section. Check the pieced Back and Front sections against the full pattern, remembering that ½" was added to the perimeter edges for quilting uptake.

Quilt Jacket Sections

13 Cut batting from the original pattern pieces, adding ½" to the perimeter for quilting shrinkage. Or use the constructed outer layer for each section, which already has the extra ½" around the perimeter.

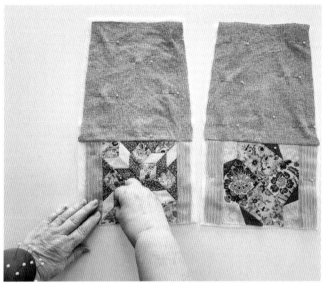

14 Stack each outer layer on its respective batting and press well. Anchor with pins or basting stitches as needed.

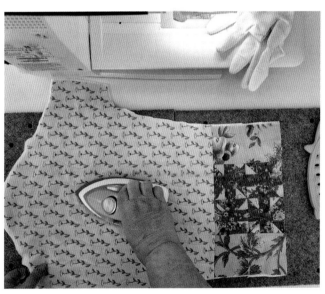

15 Quilt each section, leaving 1" all around unquilted except at the hem edge. Mark the stopping point with a preferred marking tool, if desired, before beginning to quilt. To keep this jacket lightweight, quilting was done lightly with gently curving lines that followed the fabric motifs. Press each quilted section firmly.

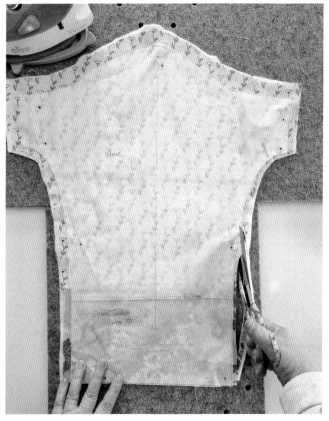

16 Place each full pattern piece on the corresponding quilted section and trim to the correct size, removing excess fabric.

Construct the Jacket

17 Assemble the jacket following Construct the Opus Jacket or Coat steps 1–6 (page 27). Make sure the hem blocks are aligned accurately at the seam lines when joining the sections together. Trim out batting beyond the seam lines at each step of construction.

18 To maintain the integrity of the quilt blocks, finish the hem with a 2" deep facing. Measure the hem circumference from one Center Front to the other. Cut a 3" wide bias or cross grain strip by the measured length.

19 Pin the hem binding, right sides together, to the lower edge of the block hem. The binding should sit snugly against the hemline, so stretch it slightly while pinning. Stitch binding in place with a ½" seam allowance. Do not remove the batting along the hem; it needs to remain to fill out the jacket's lower edge.

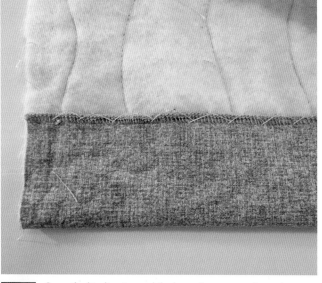

20 Press the binding toward the hem, then wrap, pin, and press the extra length to the wrong side of the jacket. Clean finish the raw edge of the binding and hand stitch the hem securely to the batting. Clean finish the raw edges of the Sleeves. Turn up hems by approximately 2" and hand stitch to the batting.

Insert Free-Hanging Lining

21 Cut out the silky lining using the full Opus pattern. To add optional cotton yokes and a back pleat to the lining, see the sidebar (page 111). Assemble the lining (step 8 of Construct).

21a Use the patterns to cut two Front Yokes and one full Back Yoke from the cotton fabric.

21b Cut two Front mid-sections from the lining fabric. Be sure to unfold the alteration that shortened the Front and Back patterns for the orphan block hem band.

Add Cotton Yokes and Back Pleat to Lining

A shoulder yoke cut from quilting cotton is a useful addition to the lining if there is not enough lining fabric, if greater support is desired in the shoulder area, or if a fabric needs to be used an additional time in the composition.

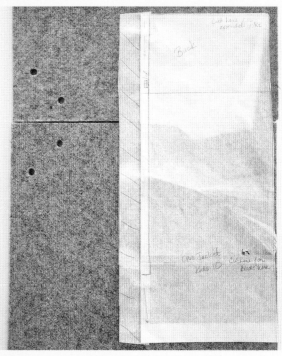

21c Add 1" in width to the Back pattern along the fold line to add the back pleat. Cut a full Back mid-section from the lining fabric that includes the pleating.

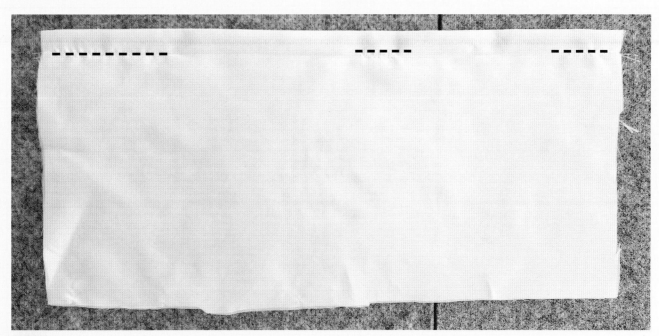

21d Fold the Back lining in half. Anchor the pleat by stitching in three places, 1" away from the fold: 3" above the hem, 2" below the yoke seam, and 1" near the waist. Press the pleat smoothly and to one side down the back of the lining.

21e Pin the Front and Back Yokes to the prepared lining sections, right sides together. Stitch a ⅝" seam, being careful to anchor the pleat smoothly in the Back-to-Yoke seam. Press Yokes away from the lower portion.

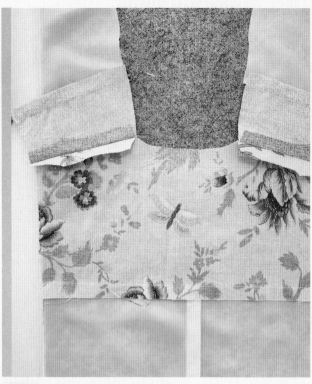

21f Finish assembling the lining (step 8 of Construct).

22 Turn the lining to the wrong side and insert it into the quilted jacket. Pin and then stitch the lining into the jacket all around the front opening, leaving the lower 2"–3" free to form a jump pleat. Tack the lining to the jacket at the shoulders and Side/Sleeve seam with thread chains.

23 Hand stitch the lining over the body and sleeve hemlines, incorporating a jump or ease pleat at each hemline (step 8 of Construct).

Add Front Band and Closures

24 Measure the jacket from center back to the finished hemline and add 2". Cut two fabric Band pieces 4¼" wide x the calculated length. Cut two batting rectangles 2¼" wide x the calculated length.

25 Hand tack the batting to the Band. Join the Band pieces at the center back by stitching a ⅝" seam along the short end, right sides together. Press seam allowances open. Press the Band in half the long way, wrong sides together.

26 Pin the batting side of the Band around the Front and neckline of the jacket, right sides together. Stitch with a ⅝" seam. Press well, and trim away the batting beyond the seam allowances. Press the raw edge of the band under by ⅝" and wrap it to the inside, pinning the pressed edge along the seam line. Hand or machine stitch in place.

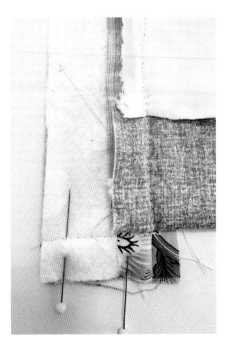

27 Finish the Band at the hems (step 9 of Construct).

28 Plan closures as desired. For this jacket, the three buttons and buttonholes were positioned around the fabric motifs on the band.

28 Quilt the band using a style that coordinates with the jacket's quilting. One softly curving quilting line runs down the center of this band and around the buttonholes. Buttons were stitched in place after the quilting was complete.

Patchwork Pattern Jacket

Size Pictured: Kids 6

This jacket was pieced from five coordinating fabrics in the Tilda Hibernation collection. The patchwork fabric was sewn with classic quilt making techniques and then quilted with a grid of lines diagonal to the patchwork squares. A silk lining is quilted in after being faced at Center Front and sleeve hems with cotton Tilda fabric. All seams and jacket edges are bound. These fine finishes create a very clean and polished interior but are time-consuming. If the faux facings at the Center Front and sleeve hem are omitted, and the seam allowances clean finished rather than bound, the patchwork jacket will still be adorable and sturdy! The jacket is closed with buttons and buttonholes.

MATERIALS NEEDED

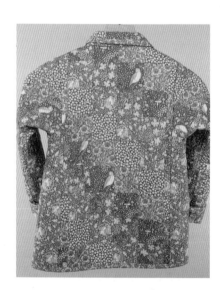

- Opus pattern, shirt collar style, jacket length

- ½ yard each of 5 or more coordinating cotton fabrics (we used Tilda Hibernation) for patchwork

- ½ yard cotton fabric (we used Slumbermouse in Lafayette) for Sides, facings, and Collar

- ½ yard cotton fabric (we used Winterrose in Sage) for binding edges of jacket

- 2–3 yards of silky fabric (we used China silk) for lining

- Batting, as needed for the selected size (we used Quilters Dream Cotton)

- Adhesive basting spray, optional

- Thread (we used Sulky 30 wt. Cotton Blendables) for quilting

- Thread (we used Gutermann Mara 100) for construction

- 4 buttons

Design Features

- **Patchwork fabric created from fabric strips and grid-style quilting.**

- **Uses a quilted-in silk lining.**

- **Buttons are used as closures.**

Create the Patchwork Fabric

Please note that the fabric created here is for a size 6 kids Opus jacket. If you are applying this method to a different kid size jacket or adult jacket, adjust the number of strips and squares.

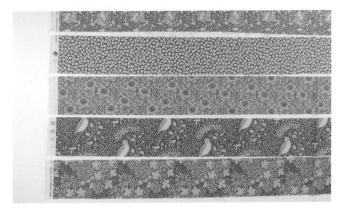

1 Cut five 3" wide strips from each of the patchwork fabrics across the width of the fabric. Lay each set of strips out in the order they are to be joined to create a set. Each set should be arranged in a different order.

2 Sew the five strips together with a ¼" seam allowance in each set. Press the seam allowances within each set to the same side, alternating right and left between the sets. For example, all seams in Set 1 are pressed to the left, all seams in Set 2 are pressed to the right, and so on.

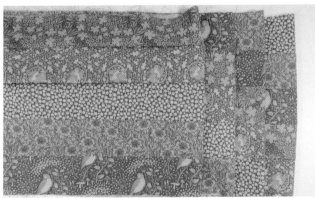

3 For this jacket, the five sets were arranged to create a diagonal pattern in the resulting patchwork.

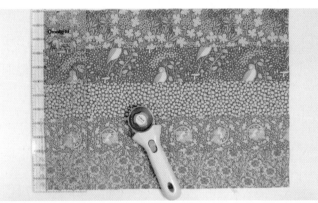

4 Crosscut each set of strips 3" wide using a rotary cutter and ruler. You may want to start by cutting only about half of each set initially, then cutting more later as needed.

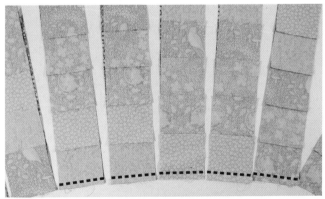

5 Lay two sets of seven crosscut strips out in the order they are to be joined, one set below the other. Sew each upper strip to a lower strip with ¼" seam allowance to create a length of ten crosscut squares. Press the seam allowances in the same direction as the others in that strip.

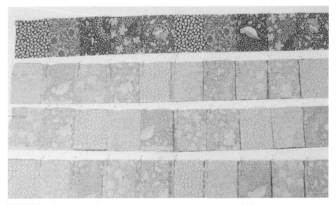

6 Pin adjoining crosscut strips together, carefully matching the corners where the patches meet and the seams intersect. At each intersection, the adjoining seam allowances should be pressed in opposite directions to reduce the bulk.

Tips for Accurate Patchwork

Here are a few tips for sewists new to piecing patchwork to make the process easier and the results more accurate:

- Use a rotary cutter, ruler, and mat for ease, speed, and accuracy when cutting and crosscutting the strips.

- Use a sewing machine foot specifically marked or designed for ¼" seam allowances if possible. Alternatively, use a seam guide or easily removable tape to mark the correct position on your machine.

- Sew slowly enough to maintain an even and accurate ¼" seam allowance.

- Press each seam allowance with a hot steam iron twice: first, lightly from the wrong side to ensure the seam is pressed in the correct direction; second, from the right side to ensure that the seam is pressed flat without any bunching or folds.

- When joining crosscut strips together, carefully match the corners where the patches meet and the seams intersect, pinning at each intersection. The adjoining seam allowances should be pressed in opposite directions to reduce bulk. If you find a corner that is off by ⅛" or more, take the time to resew before joining the crosscut strips.

- Sew carefully, making sure the seam allowances are not pushed in the wrong direction as they pass under the machine foot. When this (inevitably!) happens, take a few minutes to release enough stitches to permit you to flip the seam allowance in the correct direction and resew.

Use tape to mark ¼" on your sewing machine for consistent seam allowances.

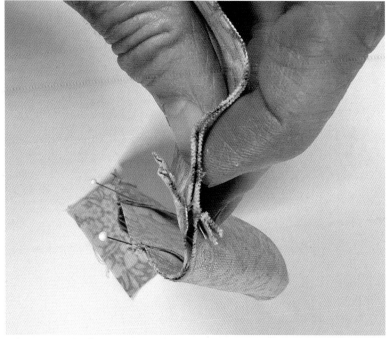

Adjoining seam allowances should be pressed in opposite directions to reduce bulk.

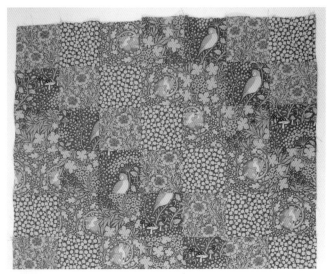

8 For the jacket Back, follow the process in steps 5–7 to create one patchwork fabric that is six squares wide and ten squares tall.

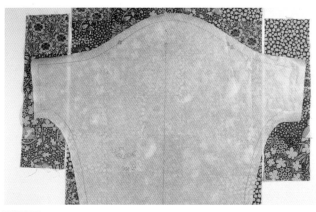

7 Sew the crosscut strips together using a ¼" seam allowance, being careful not to allow the seam allowances to be pushed in the wrong direction as they pass under the machine foot. Press all vertical seam allowances in the same direction. This patchwork fabric , 7 squares wide x 10 squares tall, is for the jacket Fronts.

9 For the Sleeves, follow the process in steps 5–7 to create two patchwork fabrics that are five squares wide and ten squares tall. Add one more strip of five squares on each side of the upper portion of the fabrics to create a seven-square-wide T shape that will accommodate the width of the Sleeve.

Prepare the Layers

10 Trace a Right and Left Front, Right and Left Sleeve, and Full Back pattern. If desired, leave an extra ½" around all sides when you cut out each traced pattern; the extra will be cut away after quilting the sections.

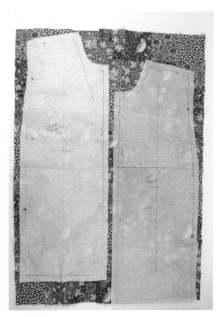

12 Cut two Side panels from the selected cotton fabric for the outer layer, remembering to cut each section an additional ½" larger on all sides to accommodate shrinkage after quilting.

11 Using the patterns, cut out the sections from the patchwork fabrics you created, remembering to cut each section an additional ½" larger on all sides. Use the patchwork seams to help you align the pattern's grainline and horizontal balance line on the fabric. Lay out the two Fronts together to make sure that the seam lines and squares match from Right to Left.

13 Cut a full set of pattern pieces from both the batting and the lining fabric. Remember to cut each section an additional ½" larger on all sides.

14 If you choose to face the Sleeve hems or Center Fronts, follow the directions in the sidebar (page 119).

Optional Facings

This jacket features optional facings attached to the lining at the Center Front, where the lining will be seen when the jacket is open, and the Sleeve hems, where the lining will be seen if rolled back to form a cuff. To add facings to your jacket, follow these steps:

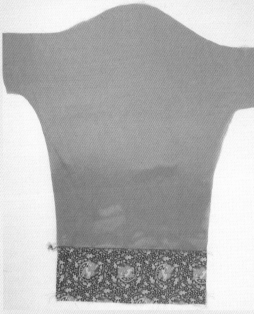

14a Measure the width of the Sleeve pattern 4" above the hem cutting line and add 1". Cut two strips of facing fabric the measured width x 3½"–4" deep. For this jacket, the Sleeve facing is cut from the same fabric as the Sides.

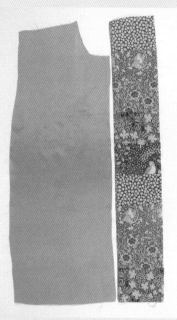

14b Measure the length of the Front pattern from the shoulder to the hem and add 1". Cut two strips of facing fabric the measured length x 3½"–4" wide. For this jacket, the facing is cut from a leftover set of joined strips, but a single fabric could also be used.

14c Clean finish the inner long edge of each facing piece by your preferred method and press. In this sample, they have been overlock-stitched with a serger.

14d Place the facing right side up on the corresponding lining piece and baste in place along the Sleeve hem or Center Front.

14e Stitch the finished edge of the facing to the lining with regular length stitches so that the facing will not get caught in the feed dogs while quilting. Turn the faced lining pieces over and cut away the facing where it extends past the lining, such as at the Front neckline.

15 Press each fabric layer in preparation for stacking. Assemble the quilt sandwiches for each jacket section with the lining right side down, batting in the center, and prepared outer layer right side facing up. Once the three layers are stacked, press the entire sandwich well, beginning in the center and radiating out.

16 Secure the layers together with pins or your preferred method in preparation for quilting. Adhesive basting spray was used to secure the layers together for this jacket because the silk lining fabric was so wiggly.

Tips for Basting with Adhesive Spray

- Choose a temporary adhesive spray labeled for use on fabrics.
- Protect your surfaces with newspaper before spraying the adhesive.
- Spray small sections at a time, a quarter to a third of the pattern piece, for better control.
- Use a weighted object, such as a ruler, to hold the unsecured sections in place as you work from one end to the other of the piece.

Quilt the Jacket Sections

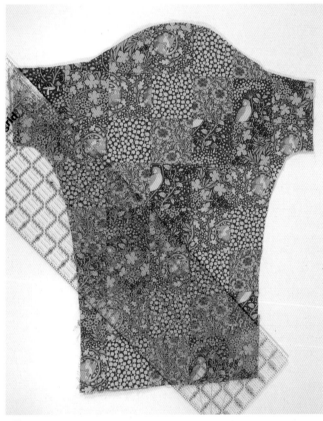

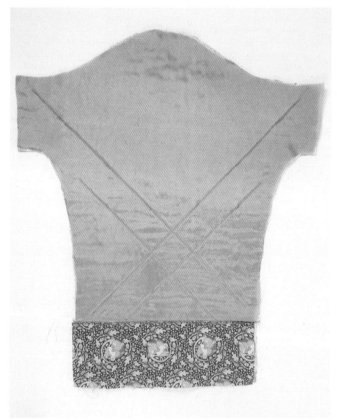

17 For each jacket section, draw two parallel lines from right to left and two from left to right in the middle of the section, passing diagonally through the corners of the square patches. Use a marking instrument that will disappear; test the marker on your quilting samples before marking the actual jacket sections.

18 Stitch along these four lines to establish the quilting grid. Remember to stop stitching 1" away from all seam edges so the batting can be trimmed out of the seam allowances later. If using a seam guide bar, use the parallel lines to secure the bar in place at the correct distance to maintain evenly spaced quilting lines. If not, use the marking tool to draw parallel lines an equal distance apart on the rest of the section.

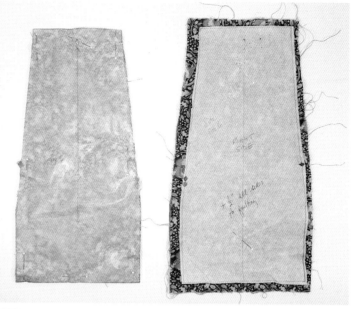

19 Sew the grid sequentially from the center of the jacket section out toward the top and bottom, alternating left and right every few lines. Press the section again after quilting is completed. Repeat this process to quilt every Sleeve, Front, Side, and Back section.

20 Lay the corresponding pattern piece on each section and trim to the correct size, cutting away the excess fabric around the edges. Use the grainlines and horizontal balance lines as a guide to place the pattern pieces correctly on the quilted sections. Don't forget to cut or mark the single and double notches on each section for easy construction.

Construct the Jacket Body

21 Assemble the jacket following Construct the Opus Jacket or Coat steps 1–6 (page 27). The following steps in this section include a few modifications to accommodate the binding.

22 Cut 1½" wide binding strips from the lining fabric. Cut strips for the shoulder seams and the Sleeve/Side seams on the straight of grain; all other binding strips must be cut on the bias. Press each strip in thirds as described for the Reversible Seam Binding Technique (page 37). This jacket utilized a total of 135" (3¾ yards) of finished binding to cover the seam allowances.

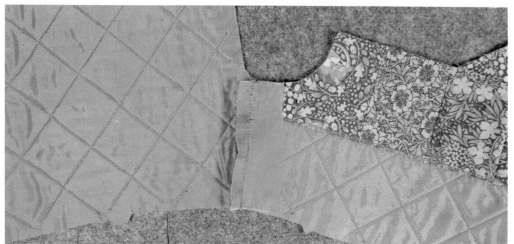

23 After sewing the shoulders together (step 2 of Construct), press the seam allowances toward the Back. Trim seam allowances to ½" and trim batting out; press again. Pin a binding strip to each shoulder seam on the Front, right sides together. Stitch with the binding against the feed dogs so you can see and follow the existing ⅝" stitch line. Press the binding toward the seam allowances.

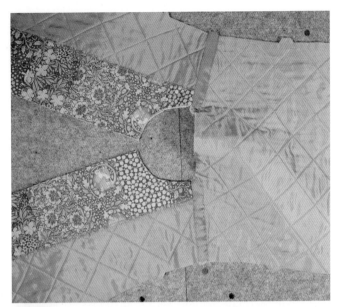

24 Wrap the final third of the binding around to cover the back of the seam, trimming and grading the seam allowances as needed to be able to wrap the binding around them. Pin the covered seam allowances to the back of shoulder and hand stitch it in place neatly and securely.

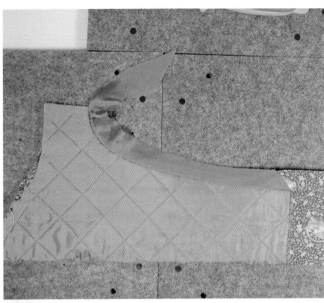

25 After sewing the underarm seams (step 3 of Construct), bind the seam allowances with lining fabric in the Reversible Seam Binding method.

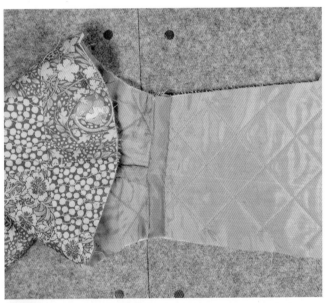

26 After sewing the Sleeves to the Side seams (step 4 of Construct), bind the seam allowances with lining fabric in the Reversible Seam Binding method.

27 After sewing the Side seams (step 5 of Construct), bind the seam allowances with lining fabric in the Reversible Seam Binding method.

Prepare and Insert Collar

28 Cut two Collars from fabric and one from the batting, remembering to leave an extra ½" on all sides; one fabric layer is cut from leftover patchwork strips and the other from cotton fabric. Stack, press, and secure the layers together. Quilt the Collar with diagonal lines, stopping 1" from the edge that will be attached to the body of the jacket. Recut the quilted Collar to fit the pattern, marking the dot on the long side.

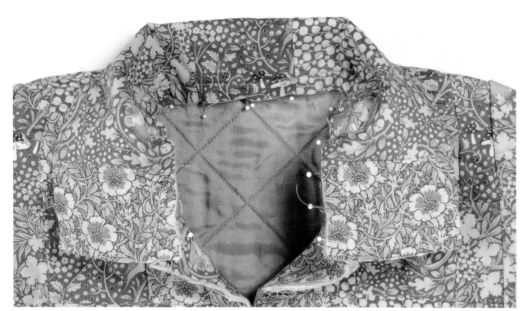

29 Pin the quilted Collar to the neckline with the patchwork side facing up. Ease the collar into place (step 10 of Construct). Pin generously to incorporate the ease along the ⅝" seam line. Baste the Collar to test the placement. Correct if needed, then sew the seam securely, backstitching at the beginning and end.

30 Trim batting from the seam allowances, grade seam allowance, and clip neckline curves. Press the seam allowances toward the collar.

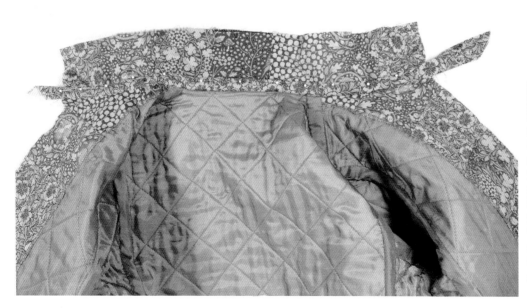

31 Cut a binding strip 1½" wide x the length of the Collar seam; this strip must be cut on the bias to curve around the neckline. Follow the Reversible Seam Binding method to prepare and stitch the binding to the back neck edge. Press the binding toward the Collar. Wrap and press the final third of the binding to the back of the seam allowances. Hand stitch the binding to the Collar.

Finish the Jacket Edges with Binding

32 Prepare ½" wide double-fold binding with 2" wide bias strips from the cotton selected for binding the jacket edges. This jacket utilizes about 100" (2¾ yards) of finished binding. All raw edges of this jacket are finished following the Classic Binding Technique (page 38).

Collar

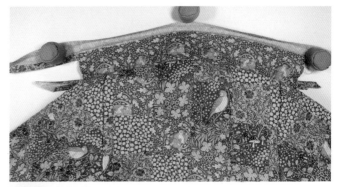

33 Measure the long unfinished edge of the Collar, and cut a prepared binding strip at this length. Pin one edge of the binding right sides together to the patchwork side of the Collar. Stitch just inside the fold. Press the binding away from the Collar. Do not trim batting out of seam allowance as it is needed to fill the binding.

34 Wrap the remaining section of the binding over the raw edges at the top of the Collar, press, and pin binding to the back of the Collar. Finish the ½" wide binding by hand stitching it to the Collar.

Center Fronts

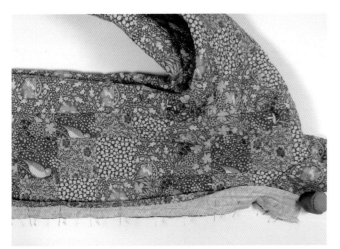

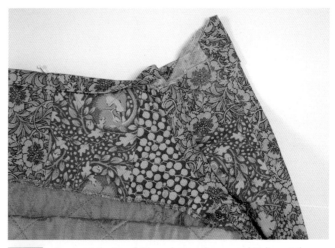

35 Measure the Center Front edges from the top of the Collar to the hem and add 1". Cut two prepared binding strips at the calculated length. Pin one edge of the binding, right sides together, to the patchwork side of each Center Front, leaving 1" of binding to extend beyond the top of the Collar. Stitch just inside the fold, backstitching at each end of the Center Front.

36 Open out the bias folds and press the excess binding at the top of the Collar, wrong sides together, even with the Collar edge. Trim the excess to ½". Refold the binding and wrap it around the edge. Press and pin the binding to the lining side. Hand stitch in place.

Hem

37 Measure the circumference of the hem and add 2". Cut a prepared binding strip at the calculated length. Pin the binding to the patchwork side, right sides together, around the hemline leaving 1" free at each end. Apply binding to the hem.

Sleeve Hems

38 Measure the circumference of the Sleeve hem and add 1". Cut two strips from the prepared binding at the calculated length. Stitch each binding into a circle with a ½" seam allowance and press the seam open.

39 Pin the binding to the patchwork side, right sides together, around the Sleeve hem. Stitch just inside the fold to secure the binding. Kids' jackets have very small Sleeve circumferences, so it's helpful to turn the sleeve inside out to stitch this seam.

40 Press binding away from the Sleeve. Wrap the binding around the edge to finish each sleeve. Hand stitch to the lining side for a smooth bound finish.

Add Buttonholes and Buttons

41 Follow steps 44–46 and 50 of Orphan Blocks Shirt Collar Jacket (page 68) to create the buttonholes and attach the four buttons. Buttons should sit within a patchwork square so the buttonhole doesn't cross over bulky seam allowances.

Reversible Vest

Size Pictured: Kids 12

This reversible vest features a group of coordinating cotton prints from the Legends of the National Parks collection by Riley Blake Designs on one side and lightweight denim on the reverse. Because it's a vest rather than an outerwear coat, it has been shortened from the child pattern's standard length. Bindings finish all seams and edges, including the vest's armhole opening. The quilting, in straight lines, follows details in the fabrics and construction.

Note: For this project, the printed side is referred to as the primary side. The denim side is referred to as the reverse side.

MATERIALS NEEDED

- Opus pattern, shirt collar style
- 1 yard of lightweight denim (8 oz. or less) for reverse side
- 1 yard of print #1 (we used Postcard Toss) for upper body and bias binding trim
- ½ yard of print #2 (we used Names in Multi) for Sides and assorted straight grain bindings
- ¾ yard of print #3 (we used Postcards in Blue) for lower body and pockets
- Batting, as needed for the selected size (we used Quilters Dream Dream Black Poly)
- Thread (we used Signature Variegated Machine Quilting Thread) for quilting
- 2 pairs of large brass snaps

Design Features

- The Sleeves of the Opus pattern are omitted for the vest.
- The Fronts and Back of the primary side are pieced along the horizontal balance line and combined with sashing.
- Kangaroo pockets are pieced and placed at the front hemline on the reverse side.
- Closes with large brass snaps.

Prepare and Quilt the Sections

1 Using the Front, Back, Side, and Collar patterns, cut a full set of denim fabric pieces. Cut a full set of batting pieces. Cut one Collar from print #1. Cut two Sides from print #2. Remember to add ½" on all sides to account for shrinkage during quilting.

2 For the primary-side Fronts and Back, which are pieced along the Horizontal Balance Line (HBL), cut as directed by the sidebar on this page.

- Fold the Front and Back pattern along the HBL.

- Cut two Upper Fronts and one Upper Back on the fold from print #1 using the pattern above the HBL (folding the pattern paper below the HBL out of the way). Add ½" on the three perimeter sides but not at the HBL.

- Cut two Lower Fronts and one Lower Back on the fold from print #3 using the pattern below the HBL (folding the pattern paper above the HBL out of the way). Add ½" on the three perimeter sides but not at the HBL. This print needs to be matched at the Center Front, so cut carefully.

- Cut 2" wide strips from print #2 on the straight of grain, which will serve as sashes connecting the Upper and Lower Fronts and Back. Two strips should be the length of the Front HBL plus 1". One strip should be twice the length of the Back HBL plus 1".

3 Using a ½" seam allowance, sew one sash to the lower edge of each Lower Front and Back. Press the sash up over the seam allowances. Attach the Upper Fronts and Back to the sashing using a ½" seam allowance. Press the seam allowances toward the sash.

4 Press all three layers of each vest section well, stacking them with the reverse-side piece right side down, batting against the wrong side of the denim, and print cotton right side up on top. Secure the layers together with pins or your preferred method. Repeat this process for the Side panels and the Collar.

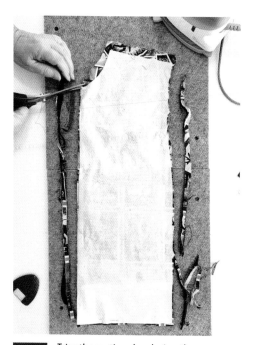

5 Quilt the Lower Fronts and Back from the primary side with lines following the postcard print design. The sashes are stitched-in-the-ditch along both seam lines. Quilt the Upper Fronts and Backs, Collar, and Sides along lines drawn with chalk on the reverse side. The star pattern in the reverse side was echo quilted above the postcard print.

7 Trim the sections by placing the corresponding pattern on each section, aligning the HBL with the center of each sash on the Fronts and Back. Pin the pattern in place and trim away any extra fabric. Cut around the notches and mark the dots on the Collar, Front, and Back where the Sides join the body.

6 After quilting each section, press well. Carefully knot loose thread tails and use a hand sewing needle to bury them into the quilt sandwich to keep them securely out of sight.

Reversible Vest **129**

Assembling the Vest

8 Pin the Fronts to the Back at the shoulders, primary sides together. Stitch the shoulder seams from the reverse side. Press the seam allowances toward the Back. Trim batting out of the seam allowances and press again.

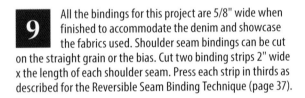

9 All the bindings for this project are 5/8" wide when finished to accommodate the denim and showcase the fabrics used. Shoulder seam bindings can be cut on the straight grain or the bias. Cut two binding strips 2" wide x the length of each shoulder seam. Press each strip in thirds as described for the Reversible Seam Binding Technique (page 37).

10 Pin a binding strip to each shoulder seam on the Front, right sides together. Sew along the ⅝" seam. Press the binding toward the seam. Trim away batting beyond the seam line, grade the seam allowances as needed to wrap the binding around, then press the binding toward the Back shoulder. Pin the binding to the back of shoulder, and hand or machine stitch it in place.

11 Attach the quilted Collar to the vest neckline with the primary side of the Collar against the primary side of the vest. This seam is stitched from the reverse side. Ease the collar into place (step 10 of Construct the Opus Jacket or Coat, page 32). Pin generously to incorporate the ease along the ⅝" seam line. Sew the seam securely, backstitching at the beginning and end.

12 Cut a strip of binding 2" wide x the length of the Collar seam; this binding must be cut on the bias to curve around the neckline. Follow the Reversible Seam Binding Technique to stitch and finish the binding on the Back neck edge. Hand stitch the binding to the Collar.

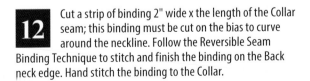

13 Cut a binding strip on the bias or straight of grain 2" wide x the length of the top edge of the Collar. Follow the Classic Binding Technique (page 38) to stitch the binding strips to the primary side of the Collar. Wrap the binding over the raw edges at the top of the Collar. Press and pin binding to the reverse side the Collar. Finish the ⅝" wide binding by hand stitching.

14 If adding the optional kangaroo pockets to the vest, follow the sidebar (page 131) instructions.

Add Kangaroo Pockets

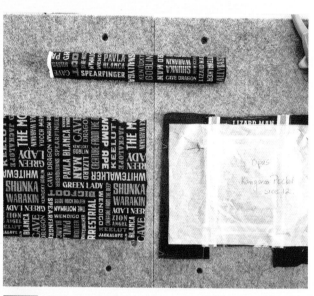

14a Create a pocket pattern piece 6½" tall x the width at the bottom edge of the Front. Adjust the height depending on the size of the vest you are making. Cut two pocket linings with this pattern.

14b Design a pair of pockets by piecing together enough fabric scraps to fill the pocket pattern; for this vest, a postcard from print #3 was cut with borders large enough to accommodate the bindings at the top and the bottom, then denim was added on each side to finish the pocket.

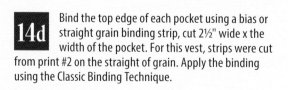

14c Stack each pieced pocket on top of a pocket lining and quilt the two layers together, repeating the quilting style used on the vest.

14d Bind the top edge of each pocket using a bias or straight grain binding strip, cut 2½" wide x the width of the pocket. For this vest, strips were cut from print #2 on the straight of grain. Apply the binding using the Classic Binding Technique.

14e Lay the pockets on top of the Lower Fronts on the reverse side, aligning the three outside edges of the pocket with the edges of the Front. Stitch around the three outside edges with a ½" seam to secure the pocket to the vest.

15 Finish the tops of each quilted Side with binding before they are inserted into the body of the vest. Cut two bias or straight grain binding strips 2½" wide x the length of the top edge of the Sides. For this vest, the side binding is cut from print #1 on the bias. Follow the directions for the Classic Binding Technique.

16 Pin each Side to a Front and Back, matching the double notches in the Back and the single notches in the Front. The primary layers are right sides together, so the seam is sewn on the reverse side. Sew each side to the body, backstitching at the beginning and end of each seam.

Tip

Because the vest has a relaxed fit and slightly extended shoulder line, decide whether this is the best positioning for the vest armhole, or if it should be narrower in the shoulder. This sample was narrowed between the armhole notches with ⅜" removed at the shoulder seam, easing back to the cutting line near each notch.

17 Measure the Side seam/armhole from hemline to hemline. Cut binding strips on the bias 2½" wide x this length for each side of the vest. Fold and press the binding strips as in the Classic Binding Technique.

18 Working from the reverse side, open the binding strip and pin to the Side seam, starting from the shoulder, continuing around the armhole, and down to the Front and Back hemlines. As it is applied, the binding should not be stretched, saggy, or loose. Sew the binding at the ⅝" seam line, backstitching at the beginning and the end. Press the binding toward the armhole/Side.

19 Follow the Classic Binding Technique to wrap the binding around the seam allowances in the armhole, pressing and pinning from the top of the Side panel at the Front to the top of the Side panel at the Back. Leave the remainder of the binding free until the next step. Hand stitch the binding to the primary side of the armhole.

20 Trim off 5/8" from the edge of the remaining binding along the Side seams. Follow the Reversible Binding Technique to bind the remainder of the Side seams down to the hem, both Front and Back. Press the bound seam toward the Sides. Pin and hand stitch the binding in place.

Finish the Center Front and Hem

21 Measure the Center Front edges of the vest from the top of the Collar to the hem and add 1". Cut two binding strips on the bias 2½" wide x the calculated length. Prepare binding using the Classic Binding Technique. Pin one fold of the binding, right sides together, to the primary side of each Center Front, leaving 1" of binding extending beyond the top of the collar. Stitch at ⅝" to secure the binding.

22 Before wrapping the binding to the reverse side, press the extra binding to the inside so it covers the Collar edge. Trim the excess to ½". Follow the Classic Binding Technique to refold, wrap, press, and pin binding to the Front on the reverse side. Hand stitch the binding to the vest.

23 Measure the circumference of the hem and add 2". Cut a binding strip on the bias 2½" wide x this length, for a ⅝" wide Classic Binding Finish. Pin the binding to the primary side, right sides together, around the hemline. Leave 1" free at each end. This binding must be gently stretched as it is pinned around the hemline to keep the edge of the vest from winging out. Sew binding at ⅝" seam line, backstitching at the beginning and end of the hemline.

24 Before wrapping the binding to the reverse side, open out the bias folds and press down the extra binding at each Center Front. Trim away extra fabric, leaving at least ½" inside the binding finish at each edge.

25 Refold the binding and wrap it around to the reverse side following the Classic Binding Technique. Confirm that the length of the Center Fronts is even on both sides. Press and pin it in place. Hand stitch the hem binding on the reverse side, creating a ⅝" wide bound edge on each side of the vest.

25 Determine the desired location of the snap closures and stitch them onto the vest.

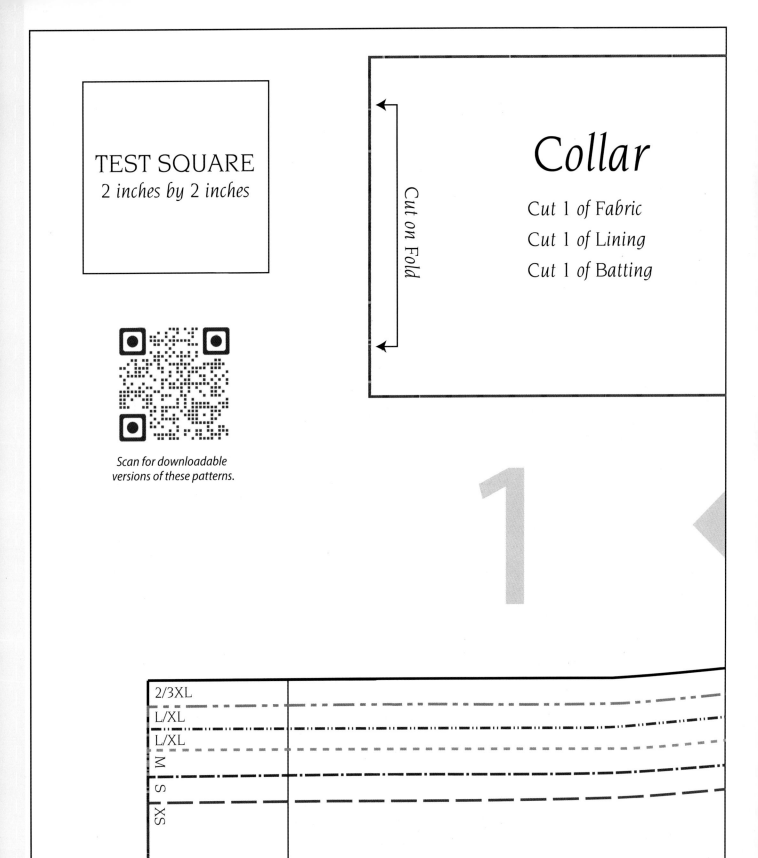

TEST SQUARE
2 inches by 2 inches

*Scan for downloadable
versions of these patterns.*

Collar

Cut 1 of Fabric

Cut 1 of Lining

Cut 1 of Batting

Cut on Fold

1

2/3XL
L/XL
L/XL
M
S
XS

Opus Jacket

by **Fit for Art Patterns**™
for Fox Chapel Publishing
©2024

XS
S
M/L
XL
2/3XL

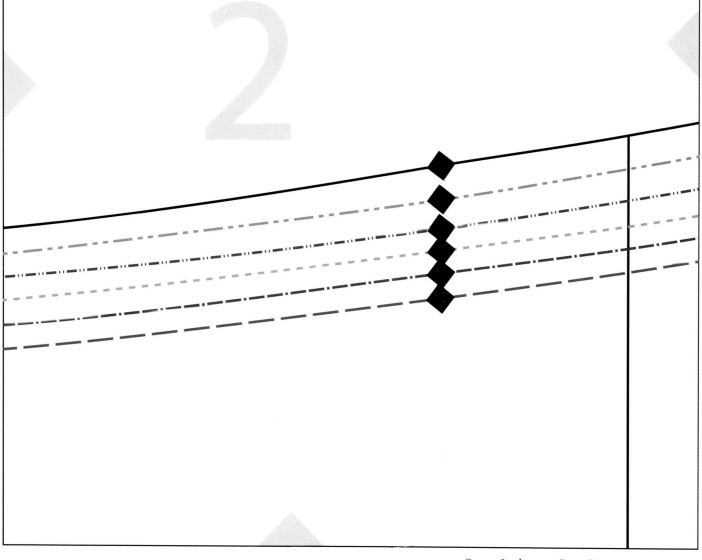

XS

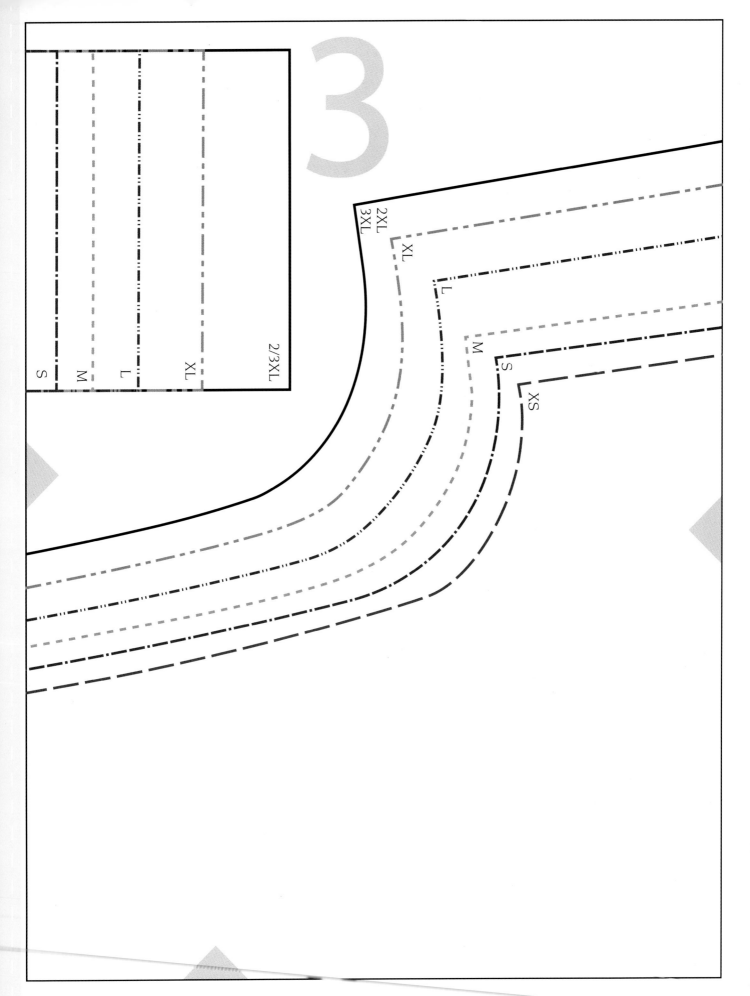

3

2XL
3XL

XL

L

M

S

XS

S

M

L

XL

2/3XL

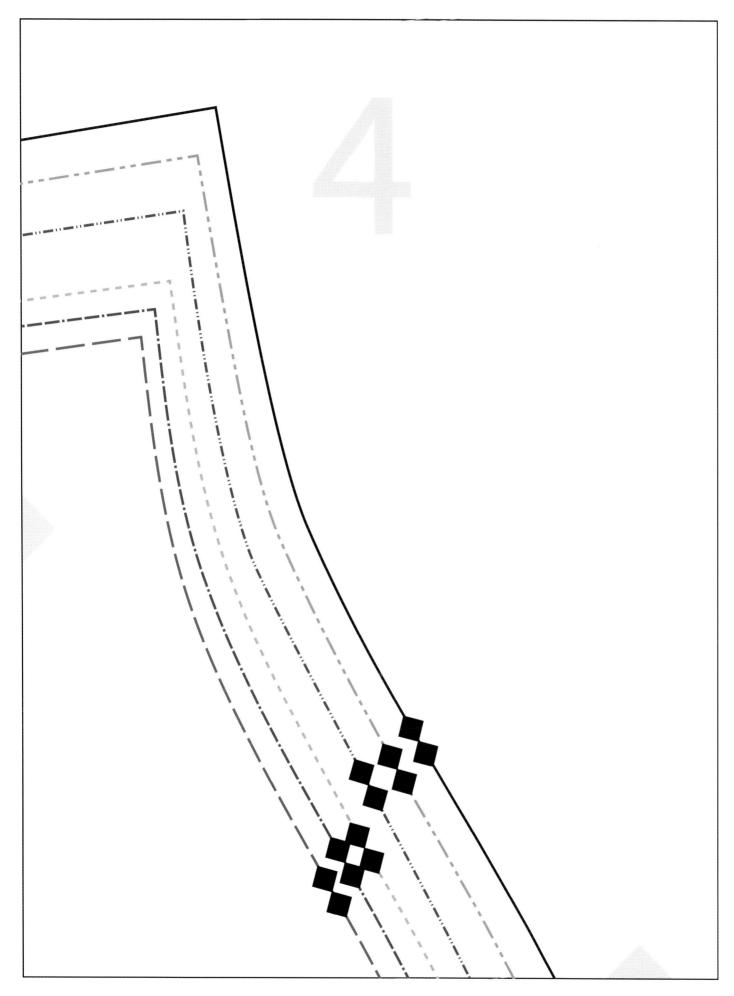

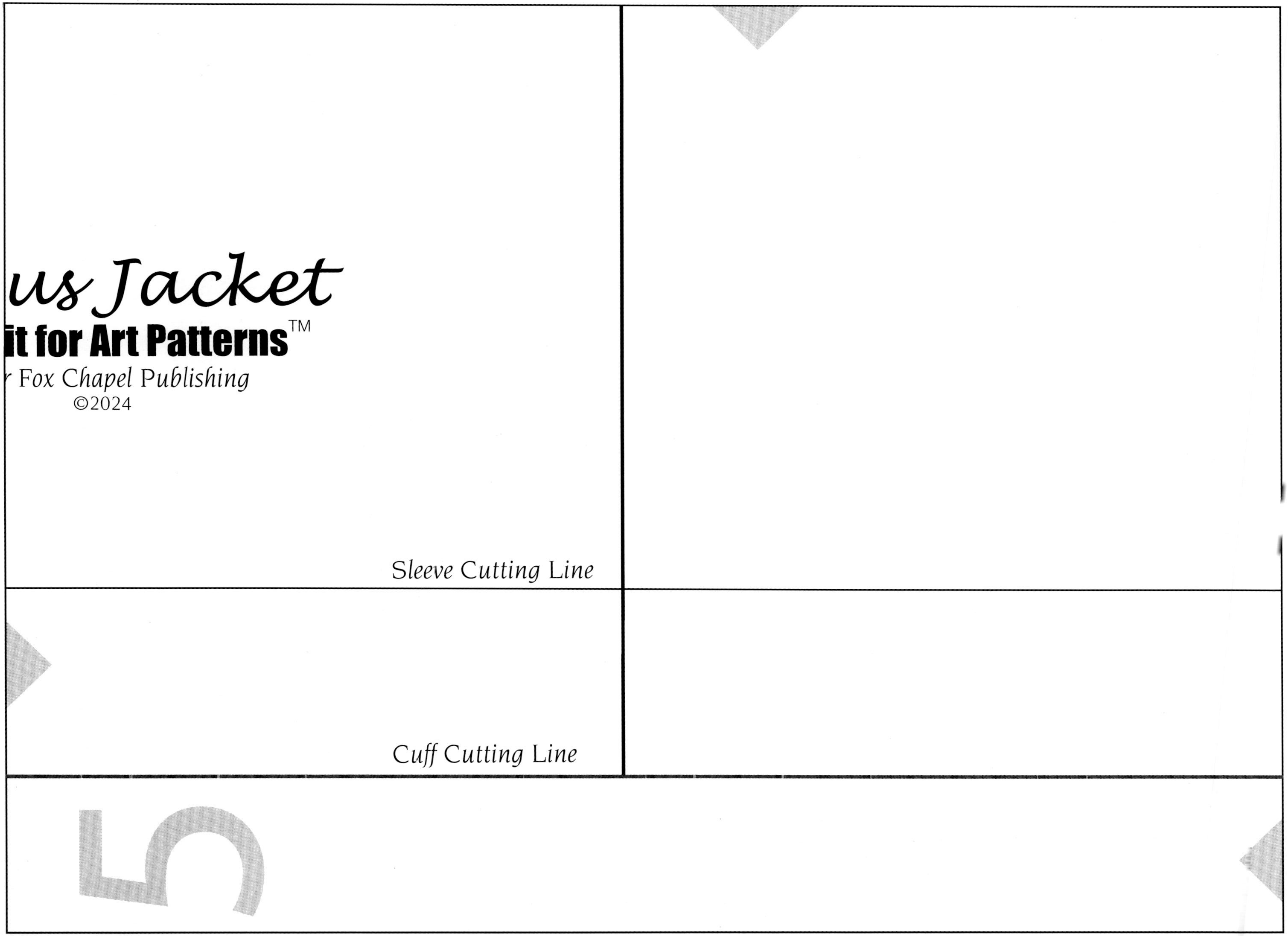

5

us Jacket

it for Art Patterns™

r Fox Chapel Publishing

©2024

Sleeve Cutting Line

Cuff Cutting Line

Grainline

Horizontal Balance Line

6

Sleeve

Cut 2 of Fabric
Cut 2 of Lining
Cut 2 of Batting

7

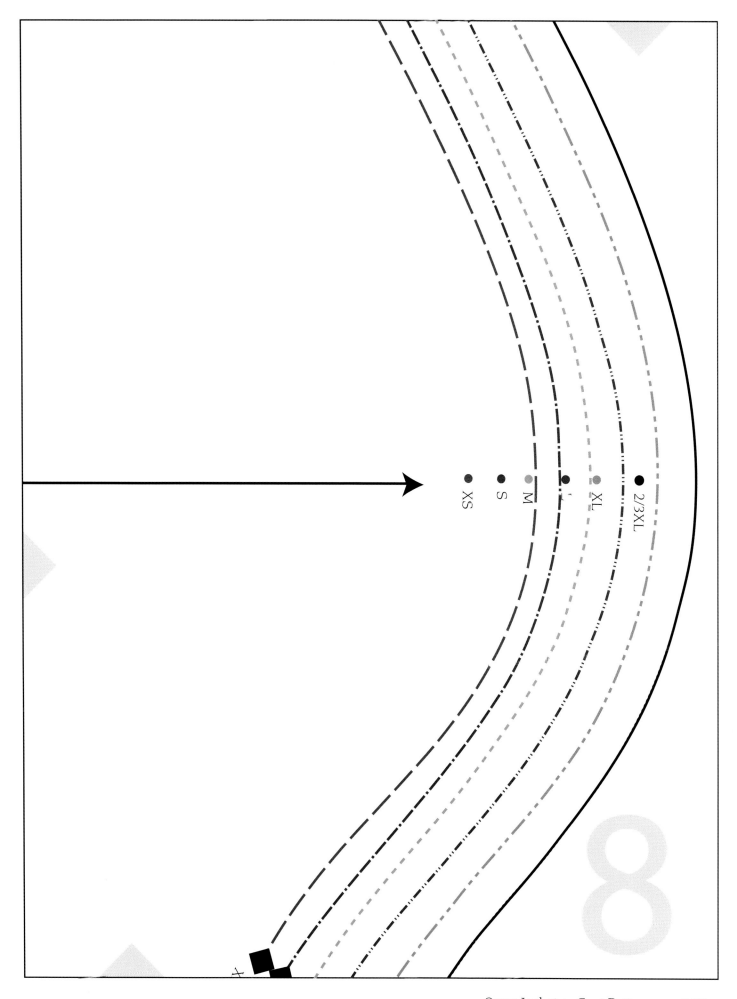

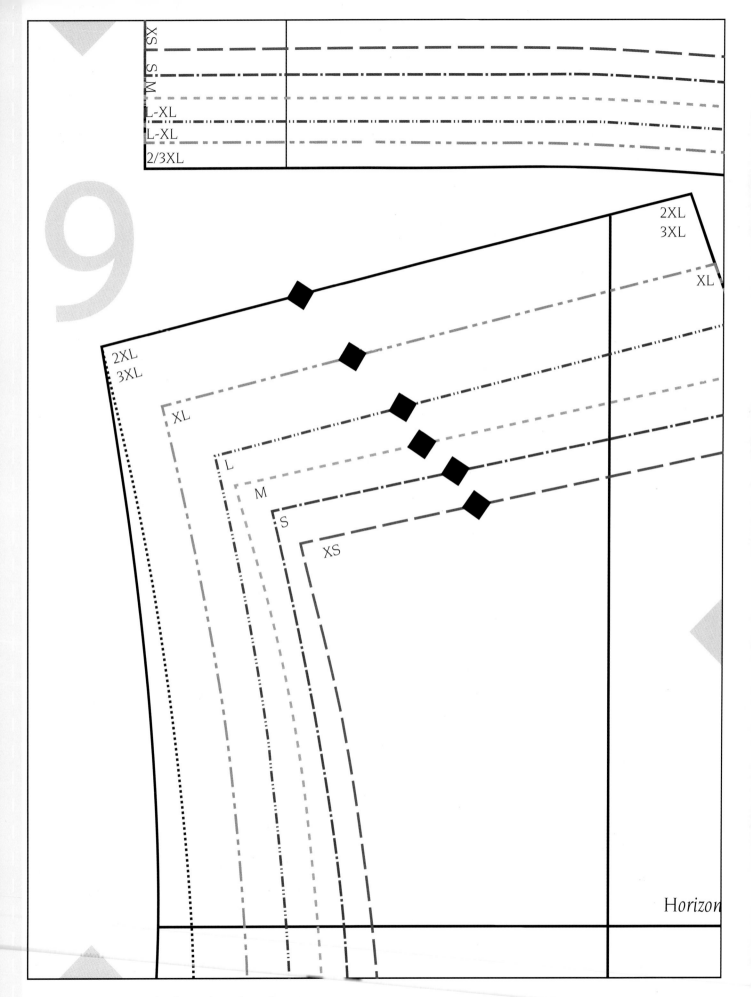

XS
S/M
L-XL
L-XL
2/3XL

2XL
3XL

XL

2XL
3XL

XL

L

M

S

XS

Horizon

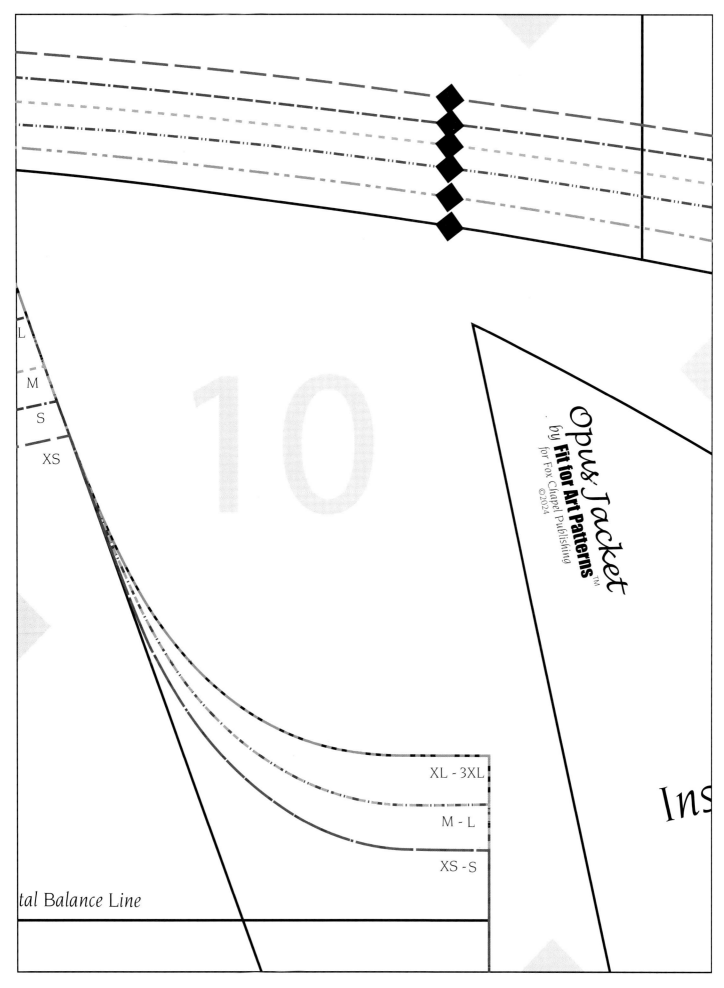

L

M

S

XS

XL - 3XL

M - L

XS - S

tal Balance Line

Opus Jacket by **Fit for Art Patterns**™ for Fox Chapel Publishing ©2024

Ins

...eam Pocket

Cut 2 of Fabric
Cut 2 of Lining

XS
S
M
L
XL
2XL
3XL

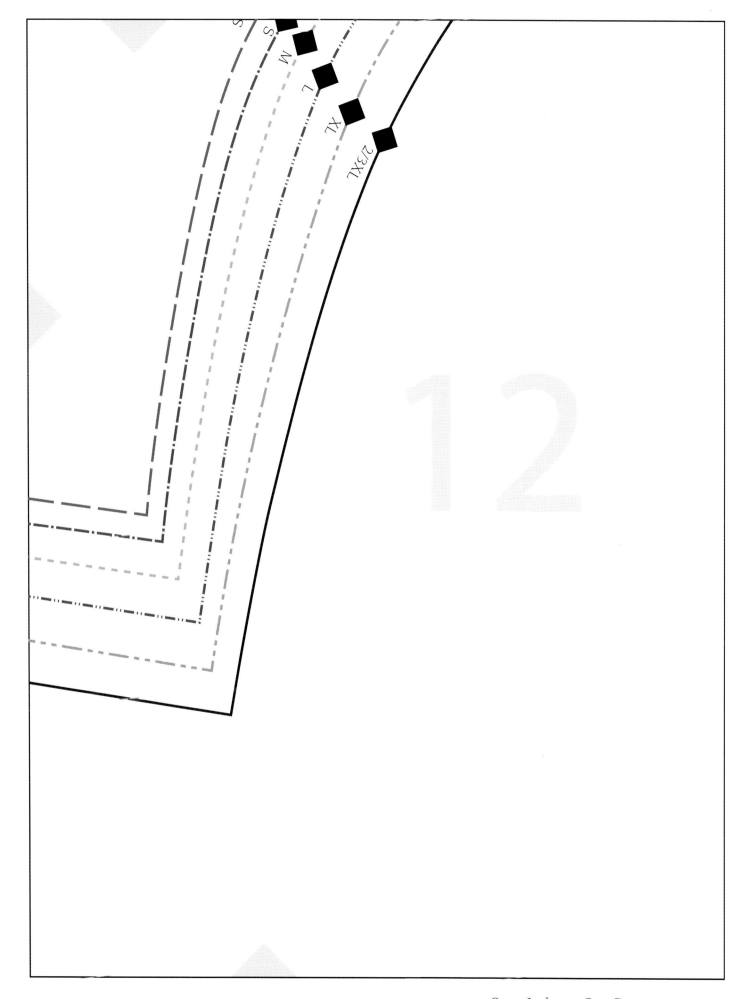

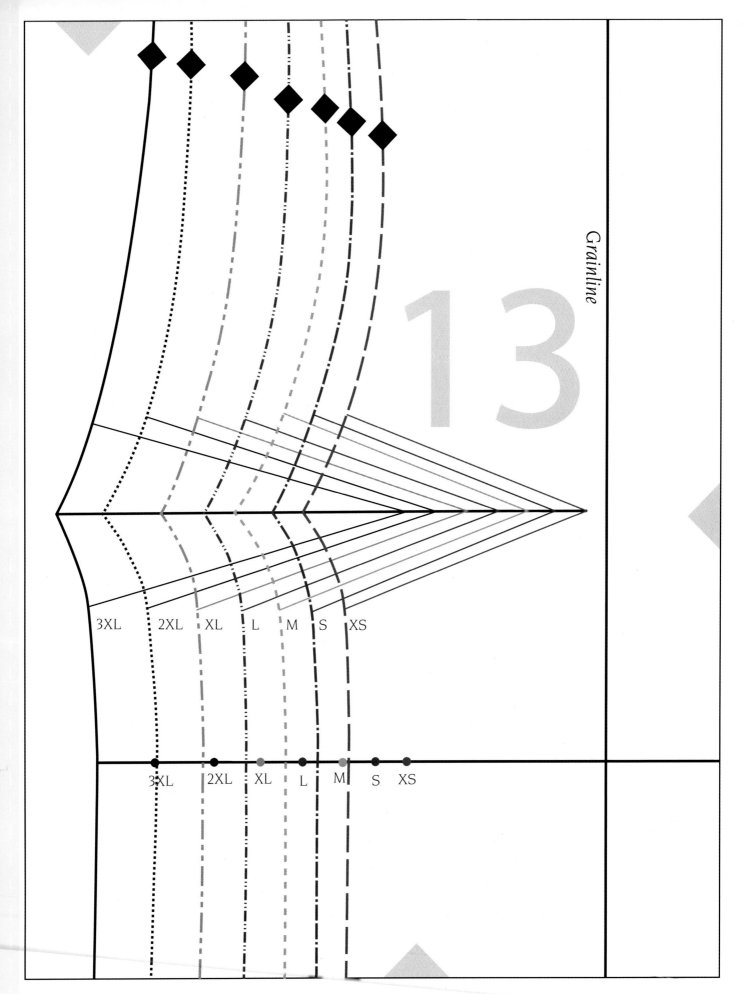

Grainline

13

3XL 2XL XL L M S XS

3XL 2XL XL L M S XS

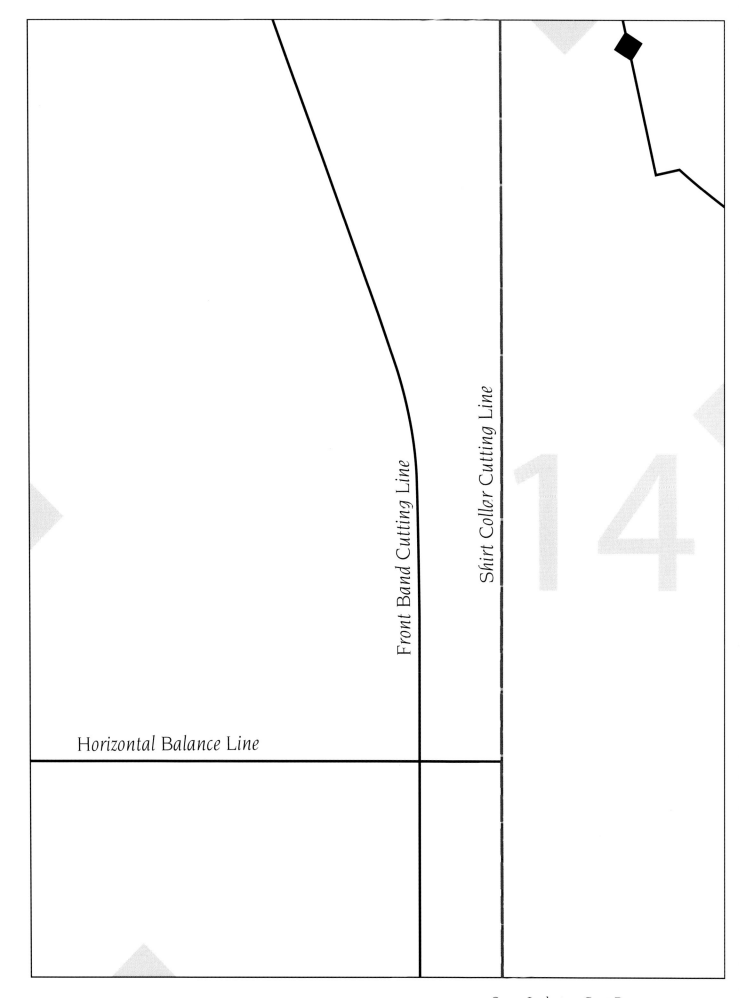

Front Band Cutting Line

Shirt Collar Cutting Line

Horizontal Balance Line

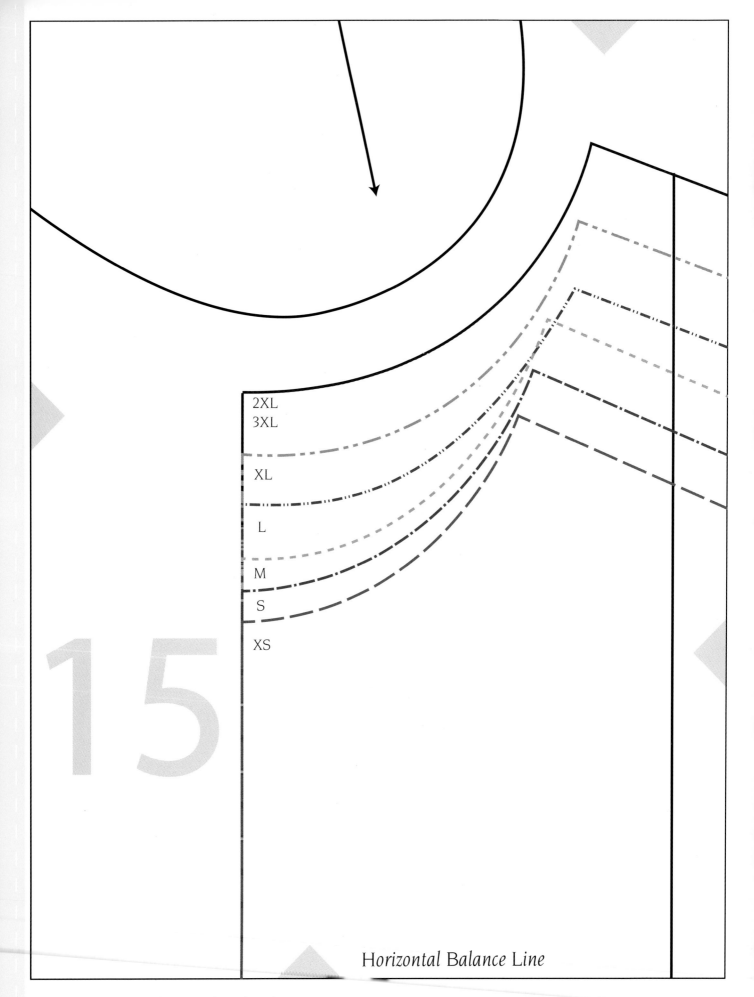

2XL
3XL

XL

L

M

S

XS

Horizontal Balance Line

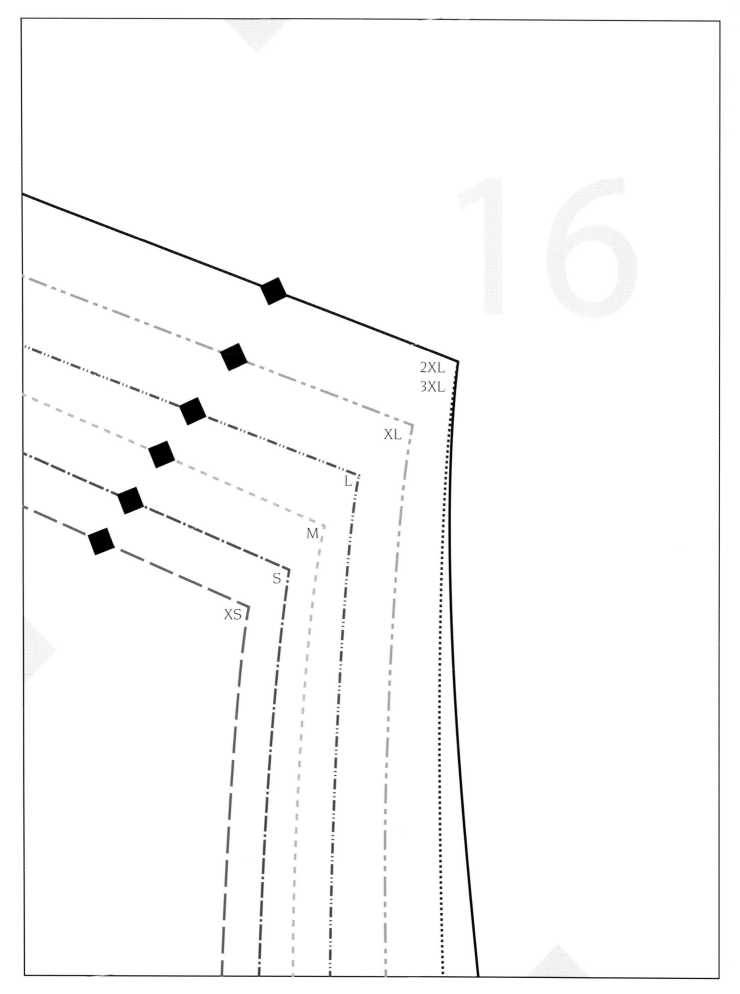

2XL
3XL

XL

L

M

S

XS

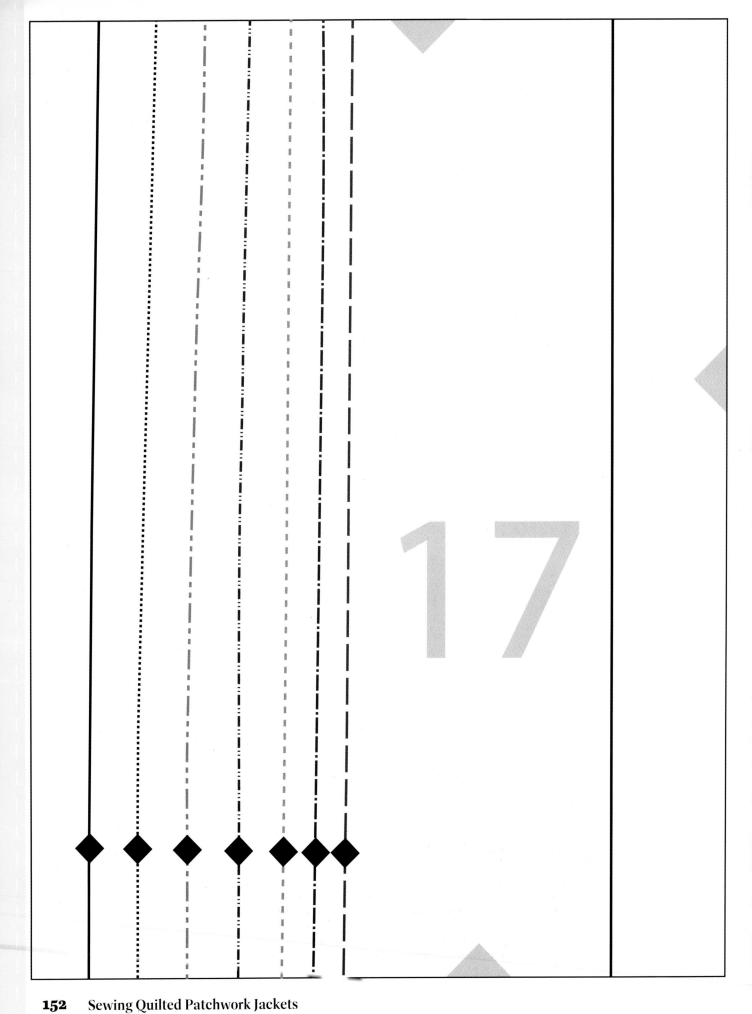

Front

Cut 2 of Fabric
Cut 2 of Lining
Cut 2 of Batting

18

Opus Jacket
by Fit for Art Patterns™
for Fox Chapel Publishing
©2024

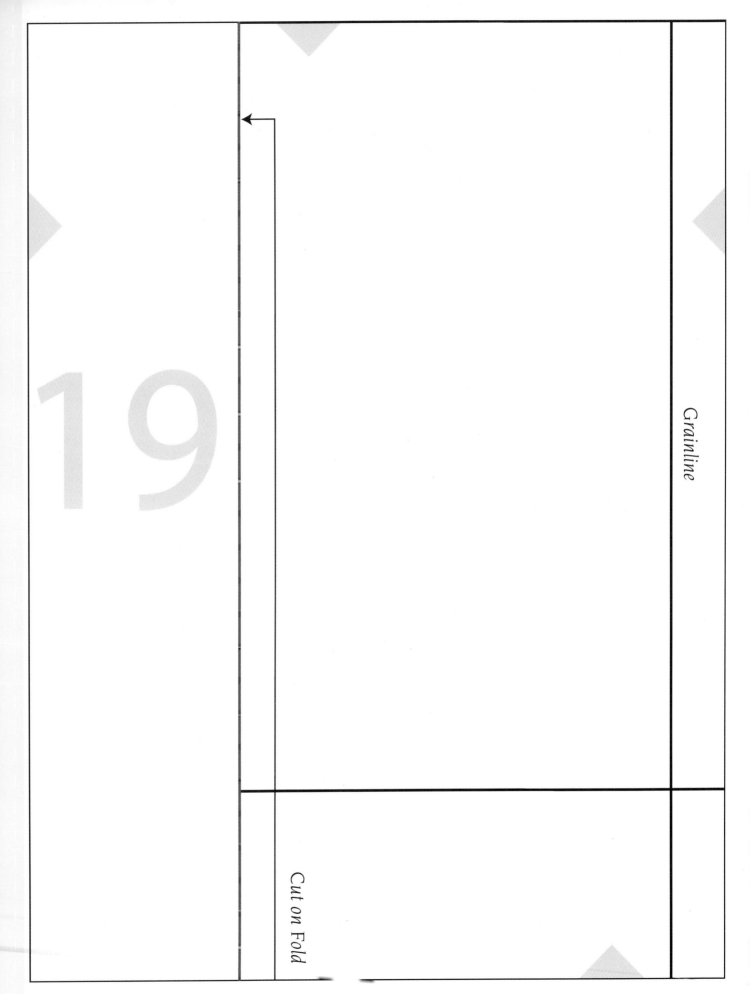

Grainline

Cut on Fold

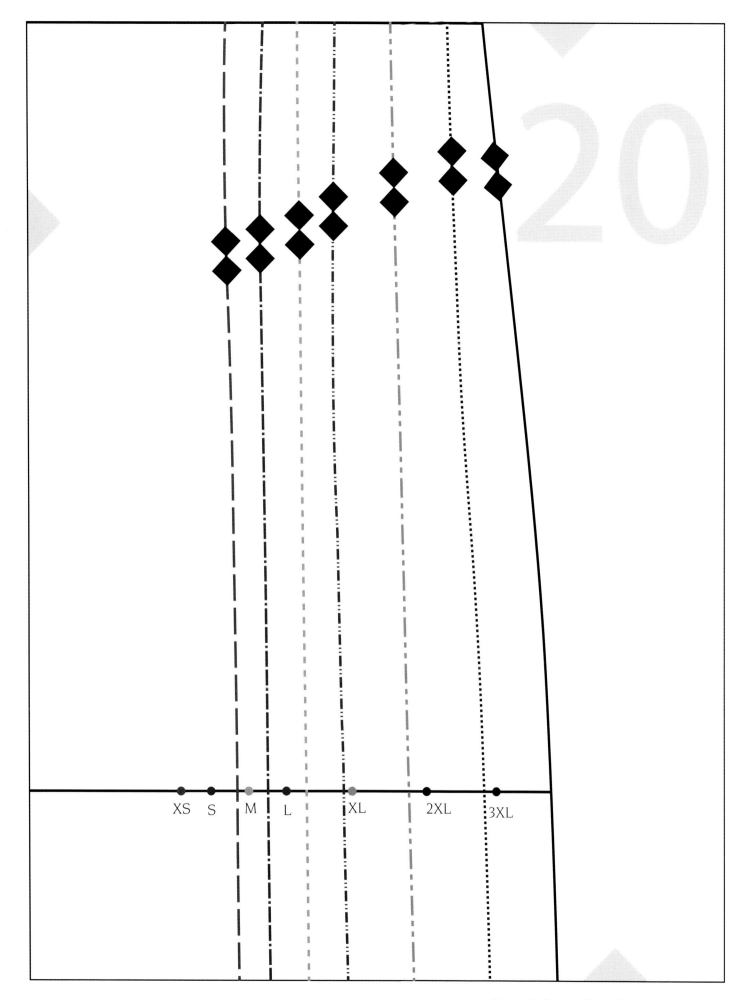

XS   S   M   L   XL   2XL   3XL

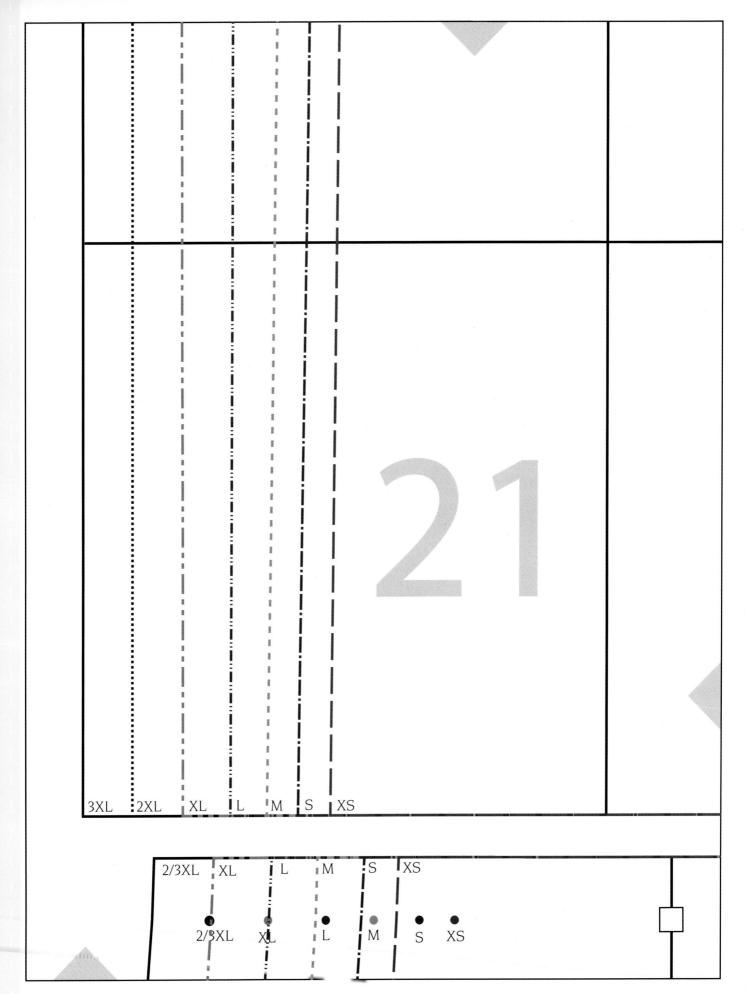

3XL 2XL XL L M S XS

21

2/3XL XL L M S XS

2/3XL XL L M S XS

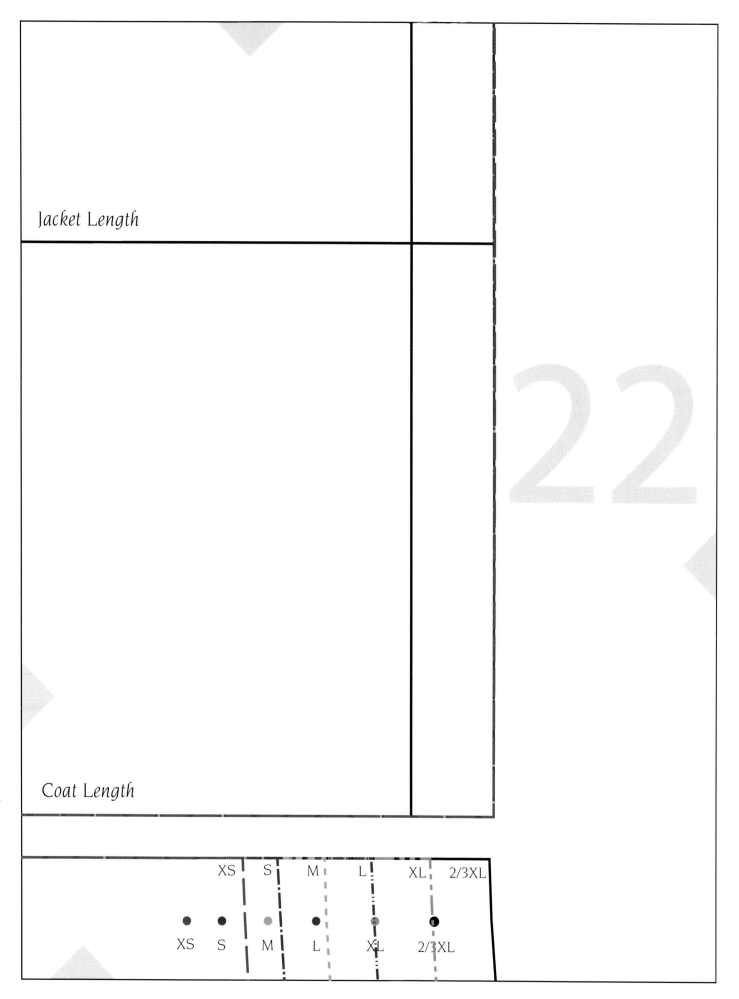

Jacket Length

Coat Length

XS   S   M   L   XL   2/3XL

XS   S   M   L   XL   2/3XL

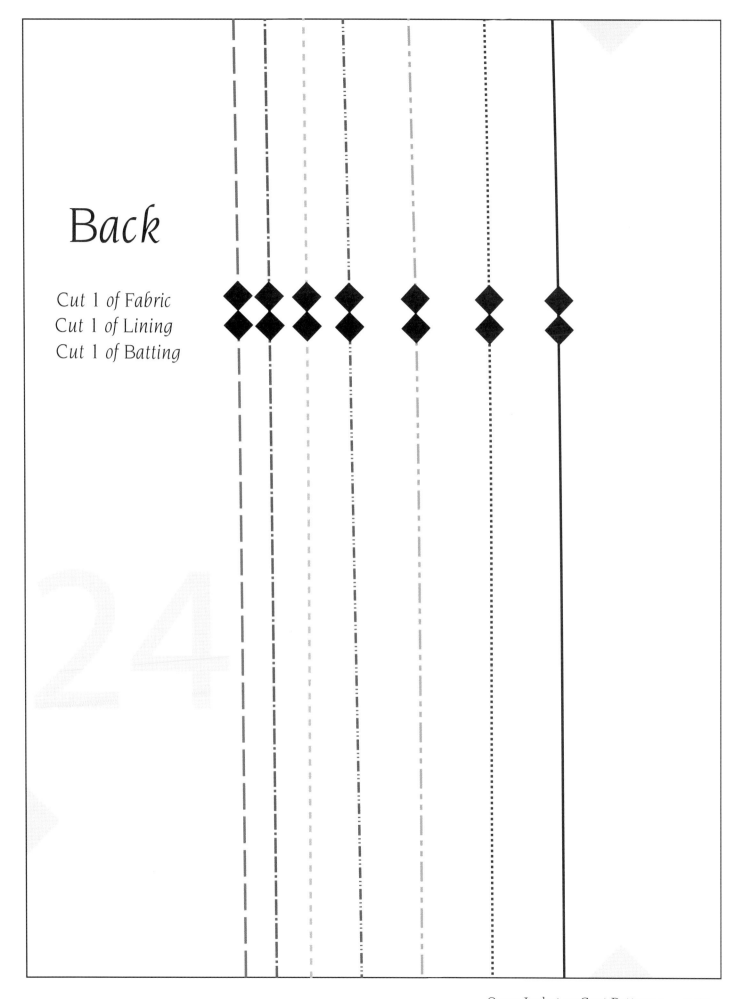

Back

Cut 1 of Fabric
Cut 1 of Lining
Cut 1 of Batting

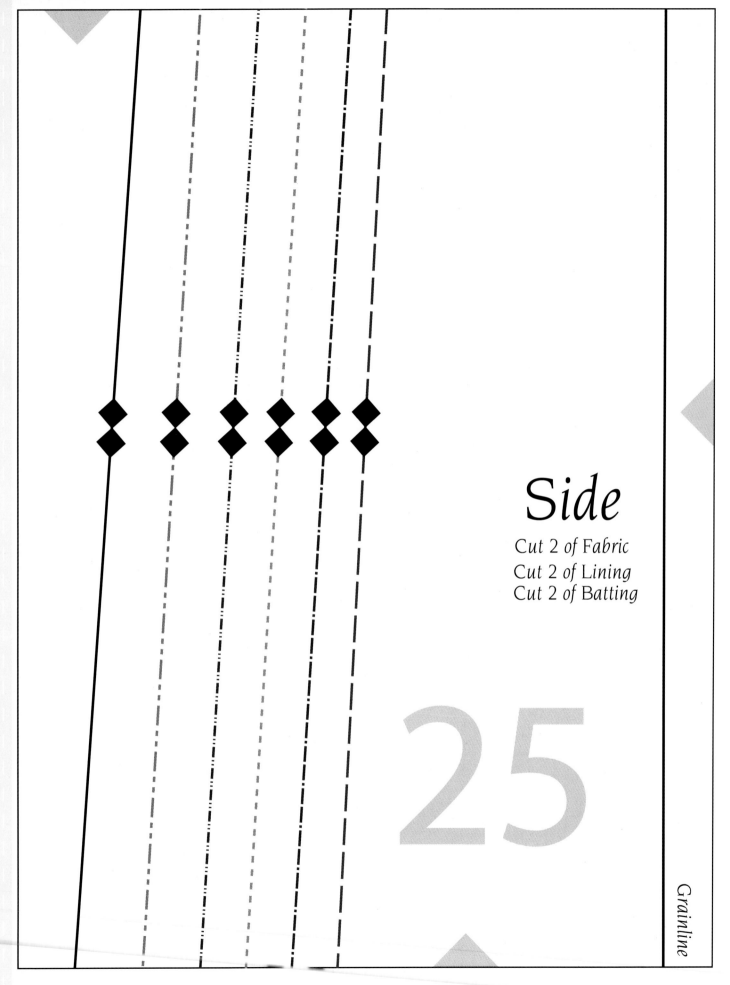

Side

Cut 2 of Fabric
Cut 2 of Lining
Cut 2 of Batting

25

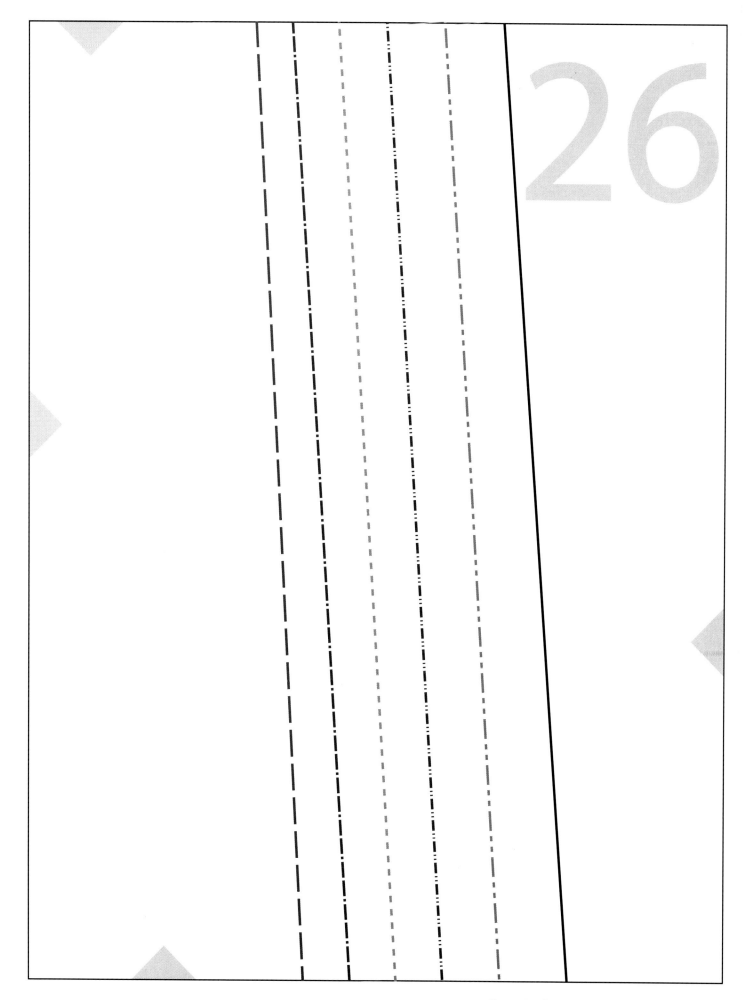

Opus Jacket
by Fit for Art Patterns™
for Fox Chapel Publishing
©2024

Jacket Length

27

Coat Length

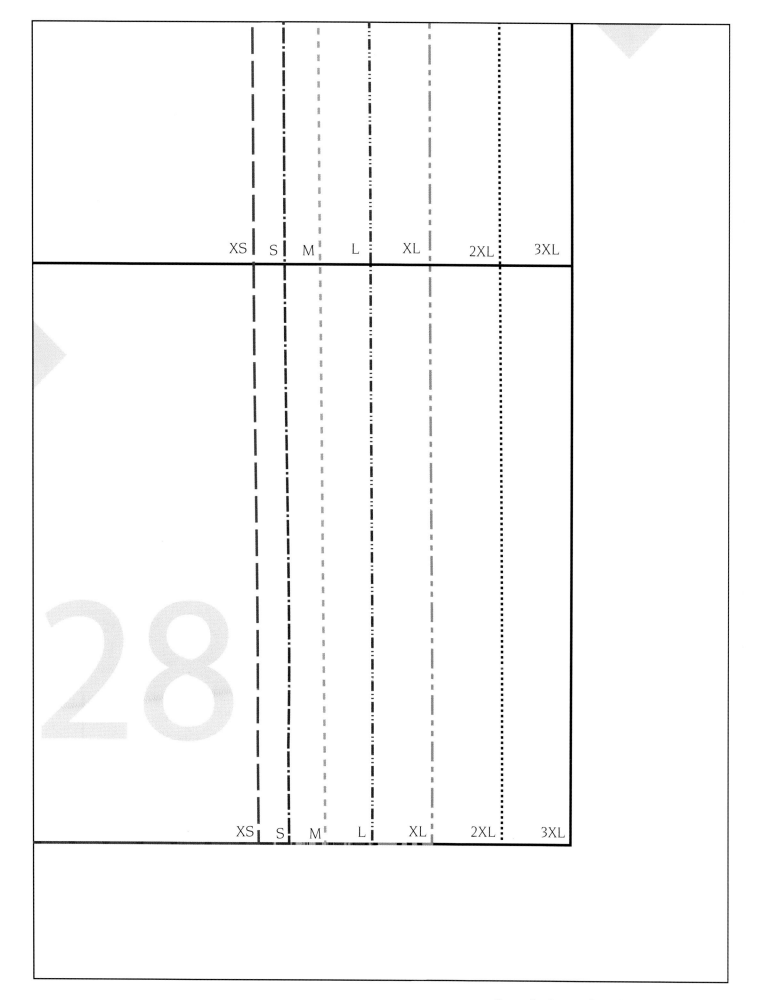

XS   S   M   L   XL   2XL   3XL

XS   S   M   L   XL   2XL   3XL

Opus Jacket
by **Fit for Art Patterns**™
for Fox Chapel Publishing
©2024

Jacket Length

29

Coat Length

2/3XL   XL   L   M   S   XS

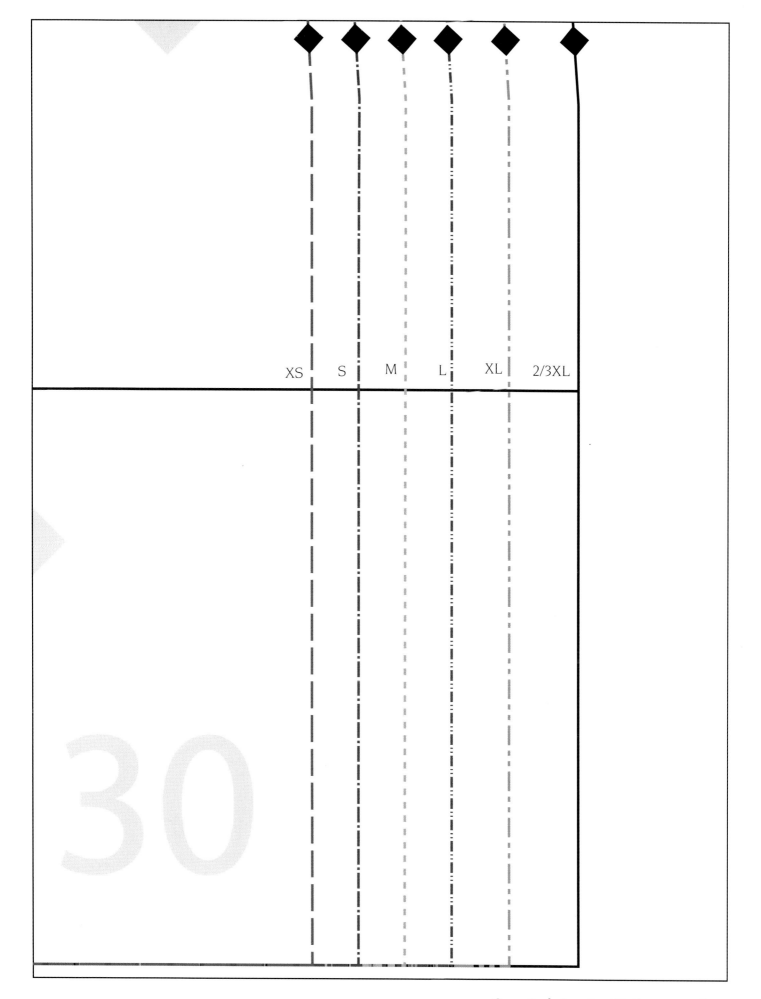

XS S M L XL 2/3XL

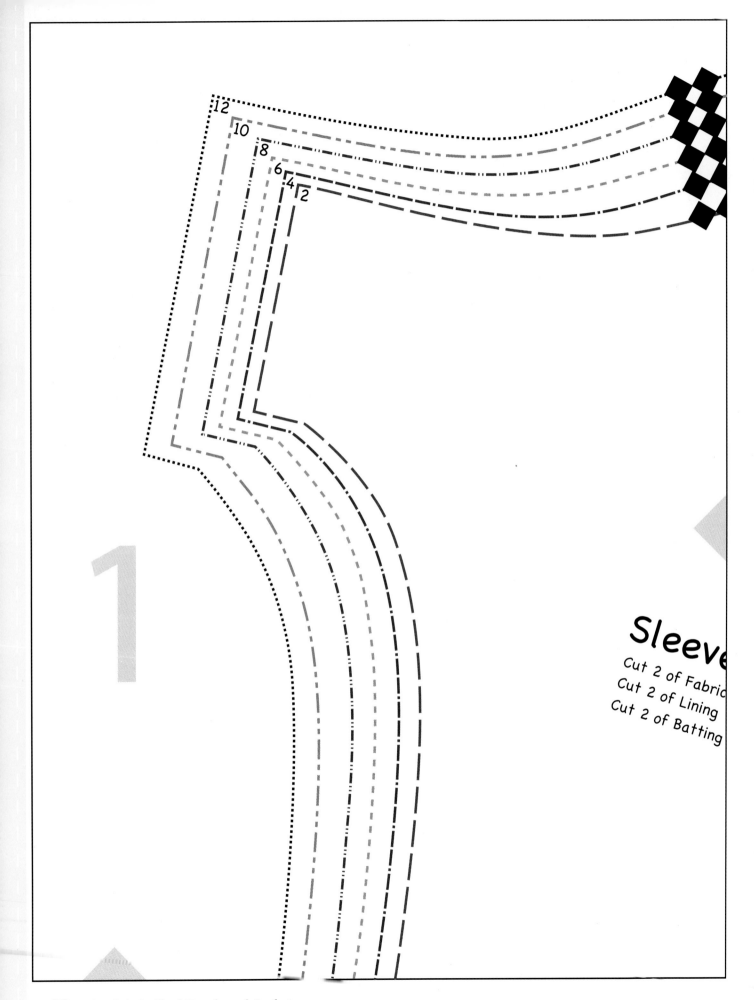

12
10
8
6
4
2

1

Sleeve
Cut 2 of Fabric
Cut 2 of Lining
Cut 2 of Batting

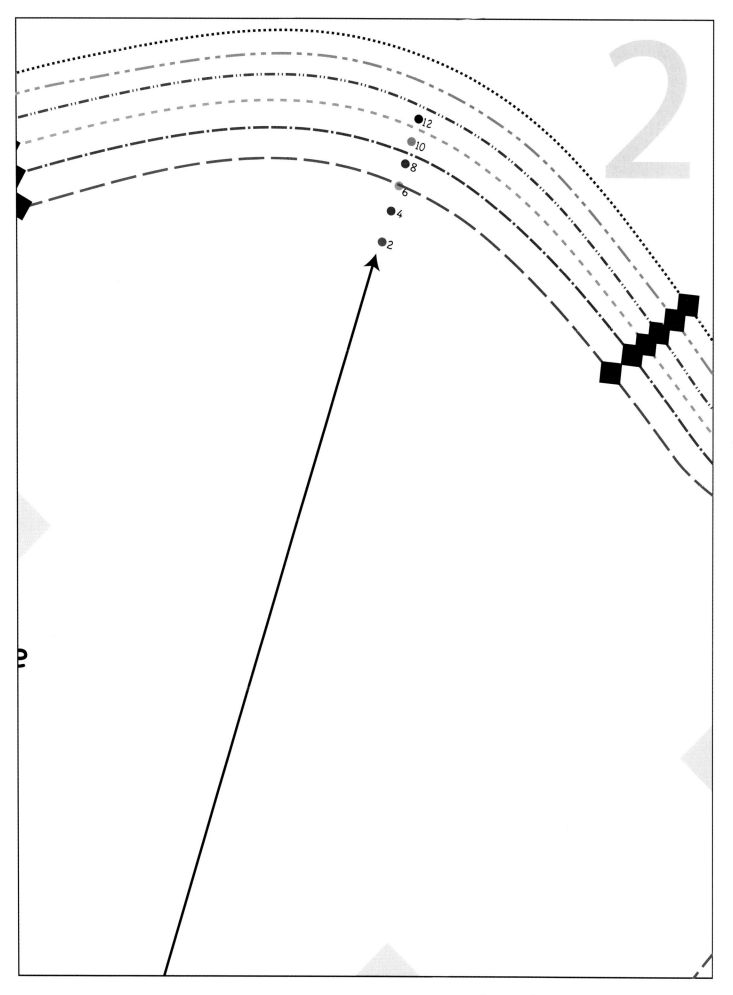

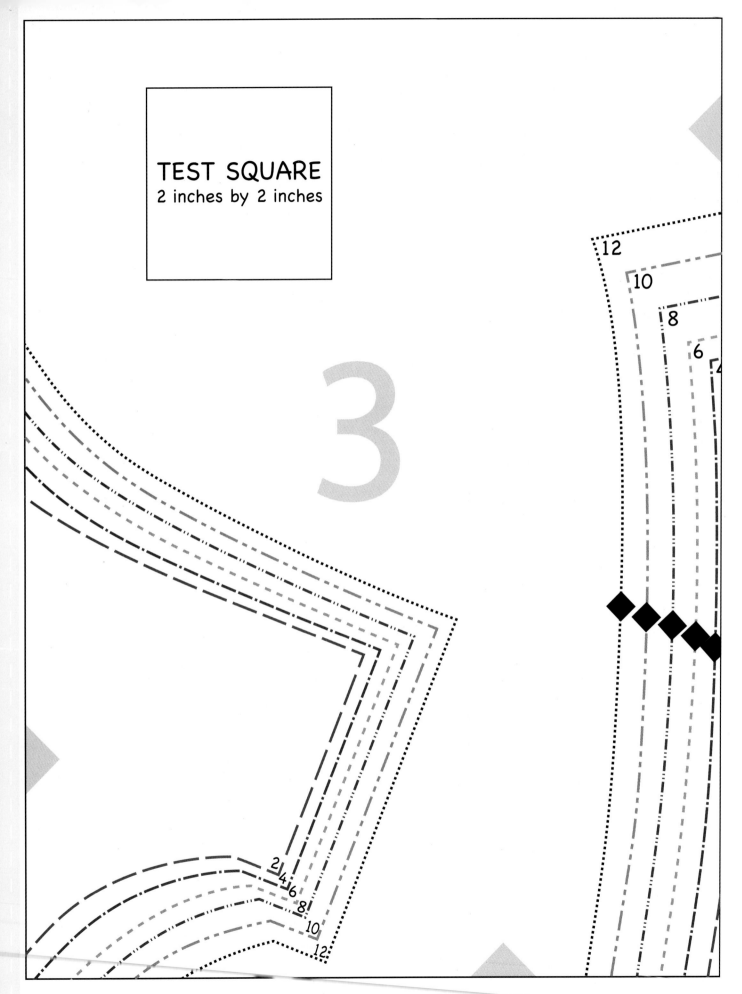

TEST SQUARE
2 inches by 2 inches

3

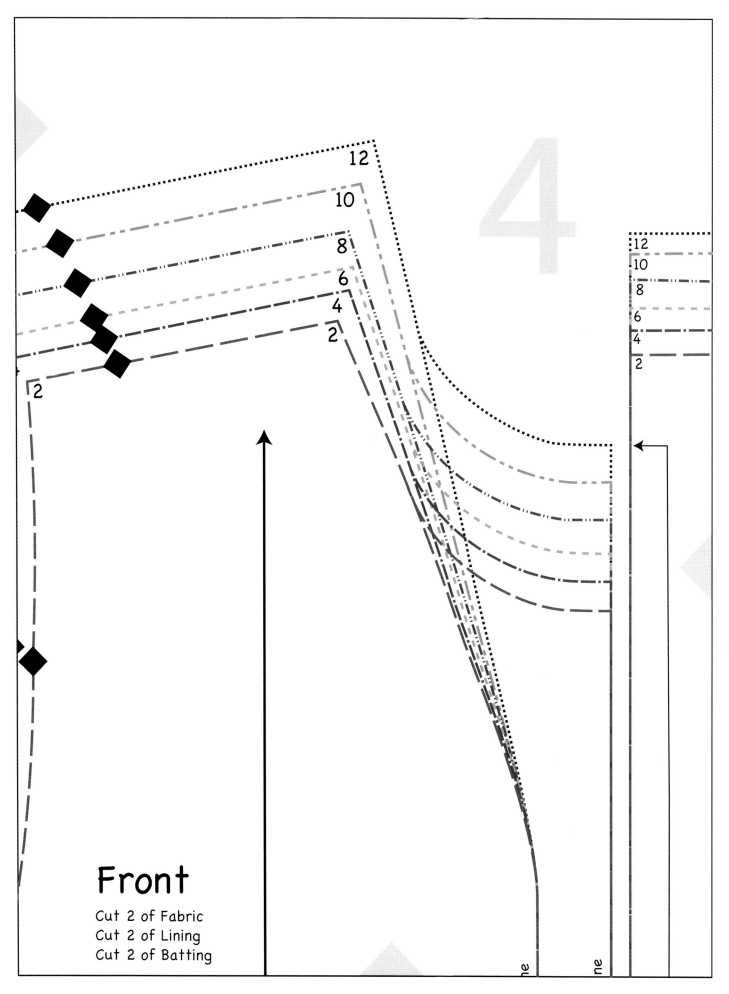

Front

Cut 2 of Fabric
Cut 2 of Lining
Cut 2 of Batting

12
10
8
6
4
2

2

12
10
8
6
4
2

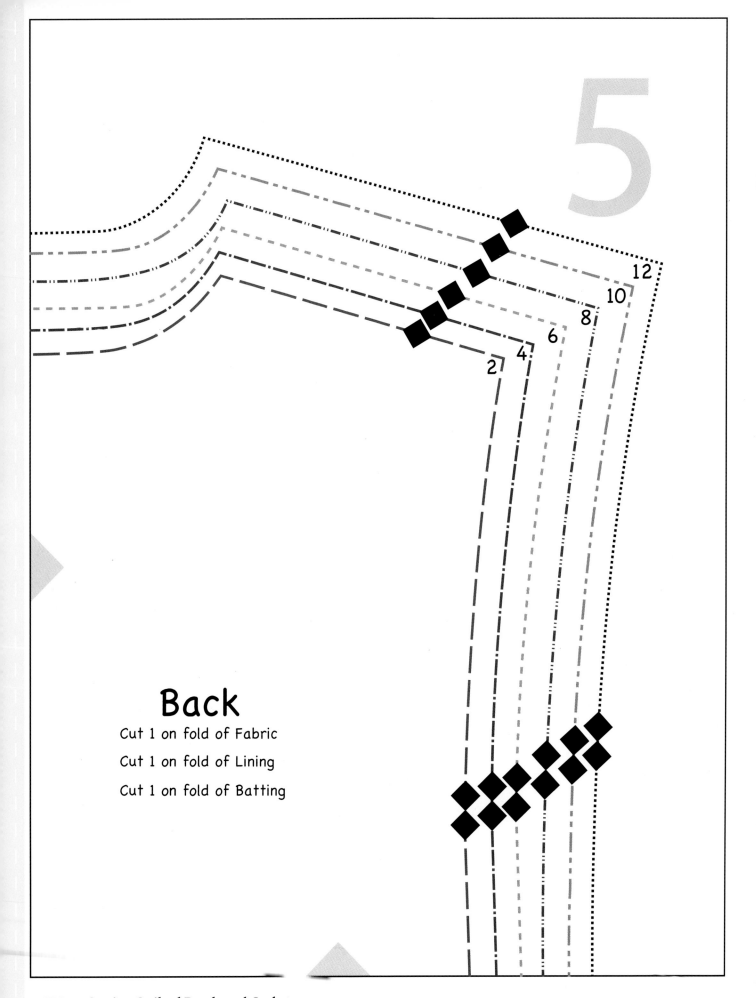

Back

Cut 1 on fold of Fabric

Cut 1 on fold of Lining

Cut 1 on fold of Batting

2 4 6 8 10 12

5

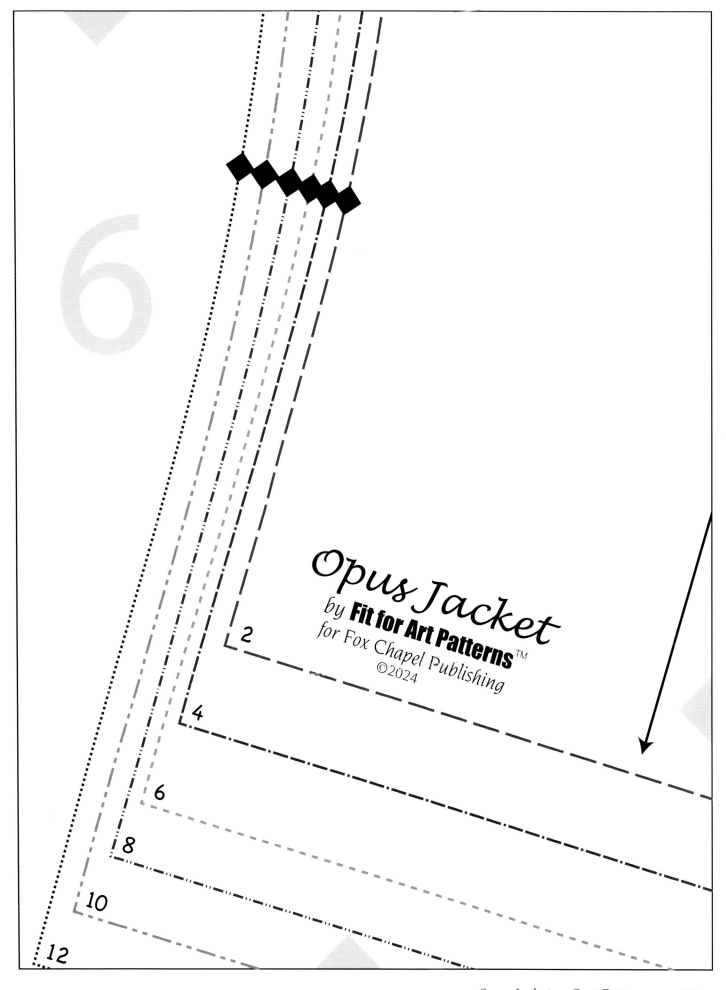

Opus Jacket
by **Fit for Art Patterns**™
for Fox Chapel Publishing
©2024

6

2

4

6

8

10

12

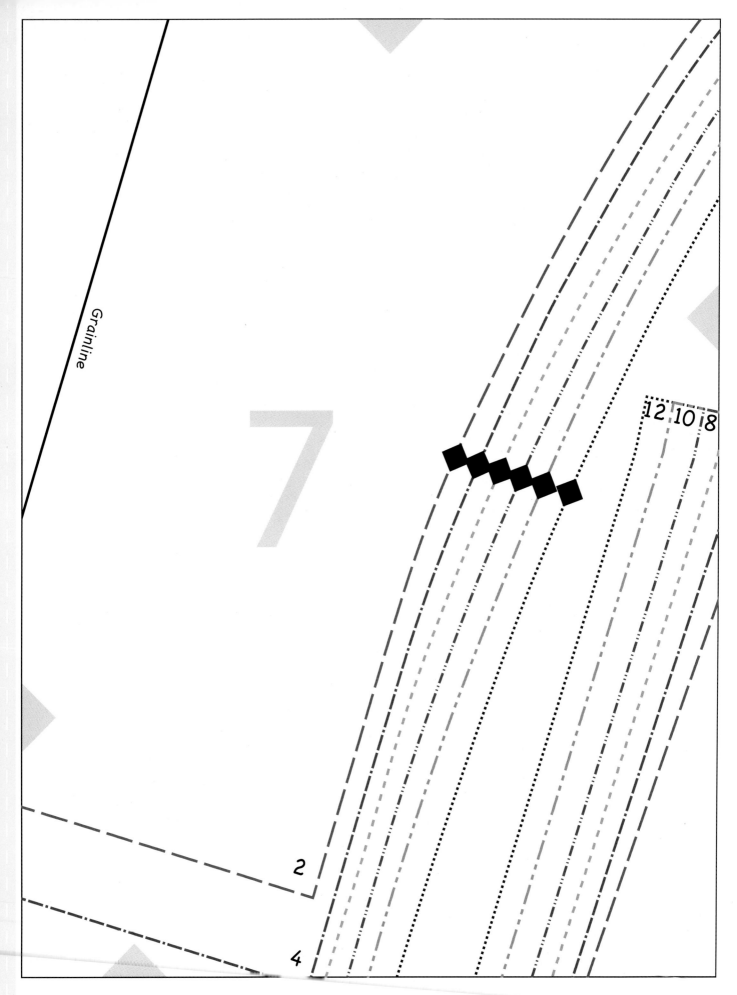

Grainline

7

12 10 8

2

4

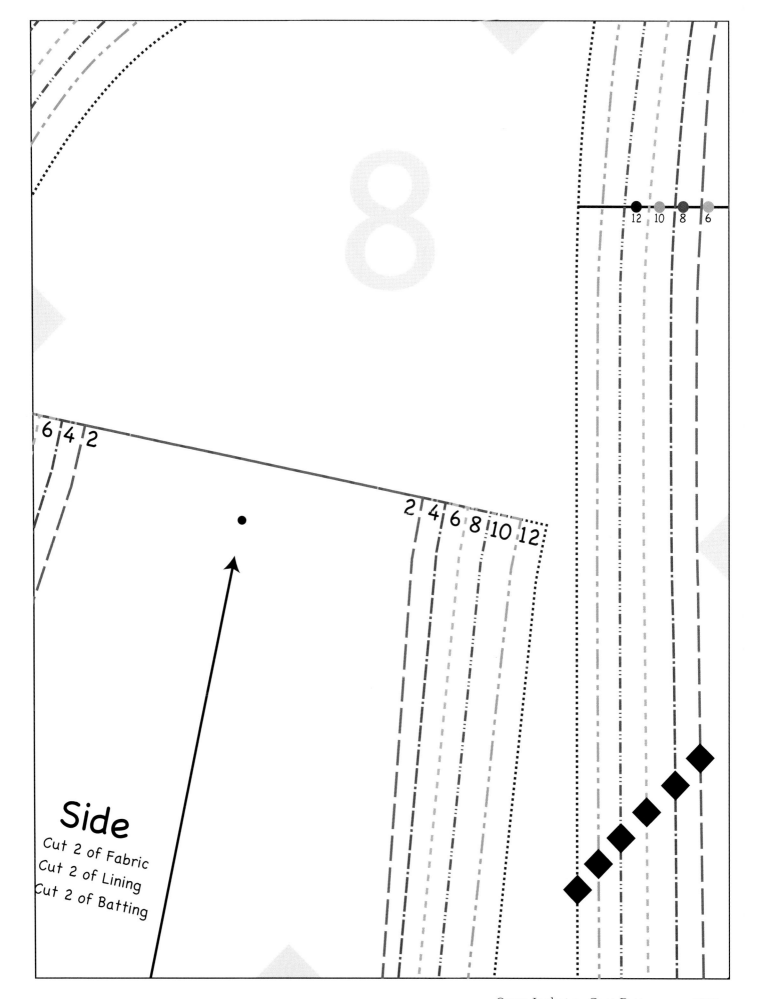

8

6 4 2

2 4 6 8 10 12

12 10 8 6

Side

Cut 2 of Fabric
Cut 2 of Lining
Cut 2 of Batting

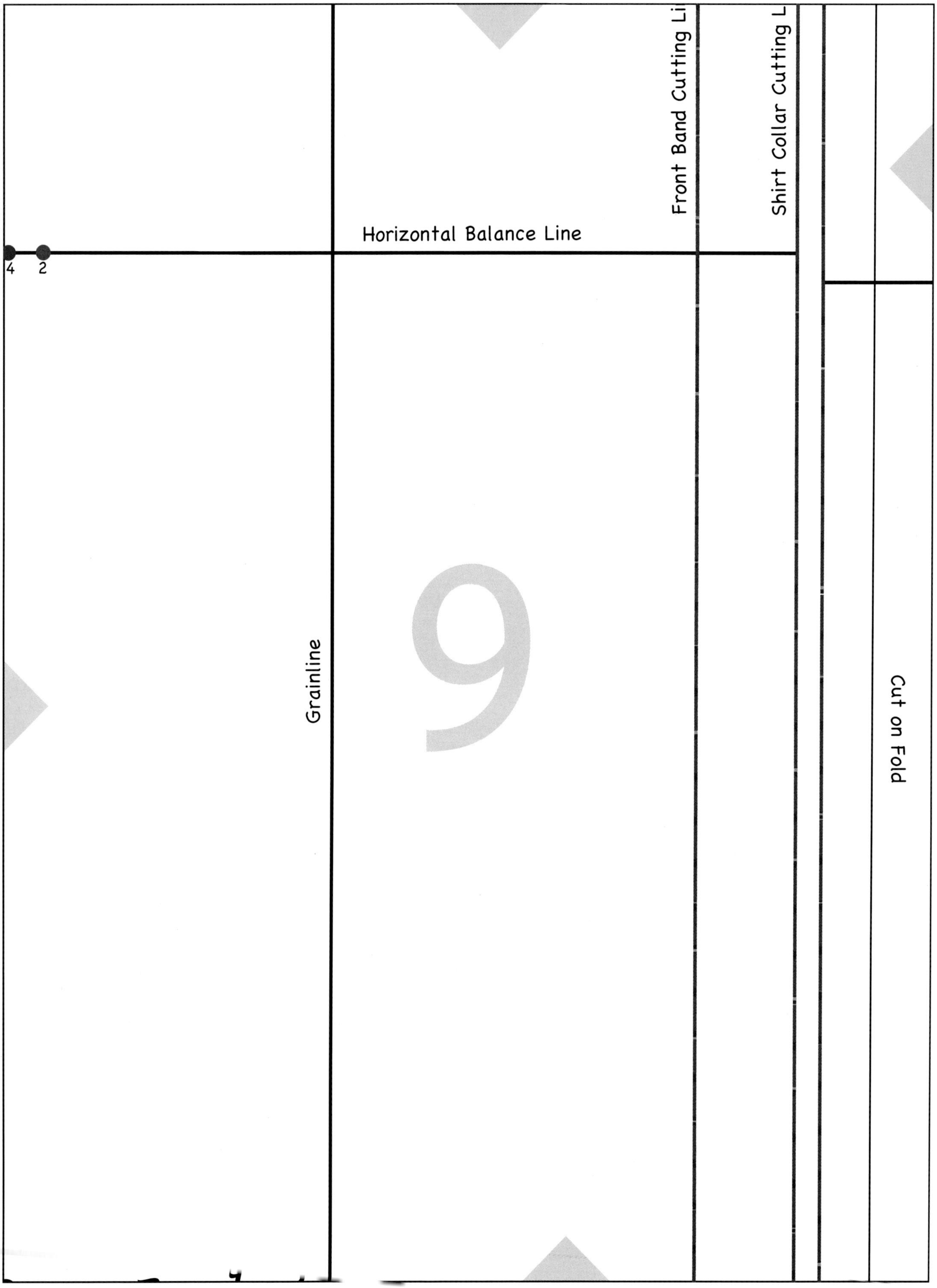

Front Band Cutting Li

Shirt Collar Cutting L

Horizontal Balance Line

4 2

Grainline

9

Cut on Fold

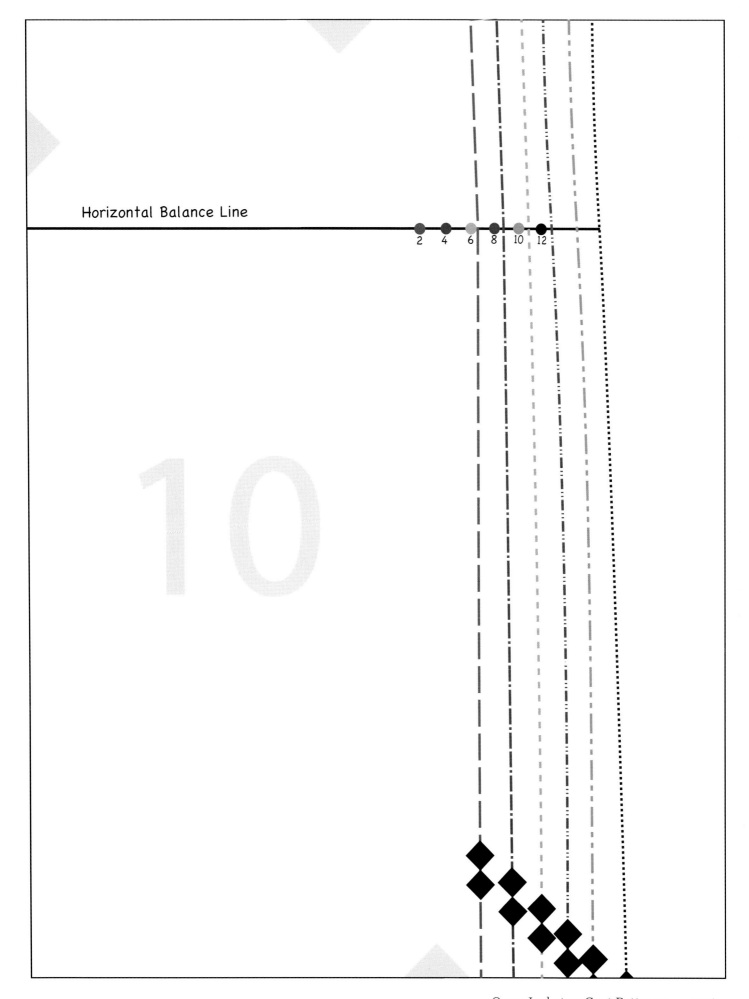

Horizontal Balance Line

2 4 6 8 10 12

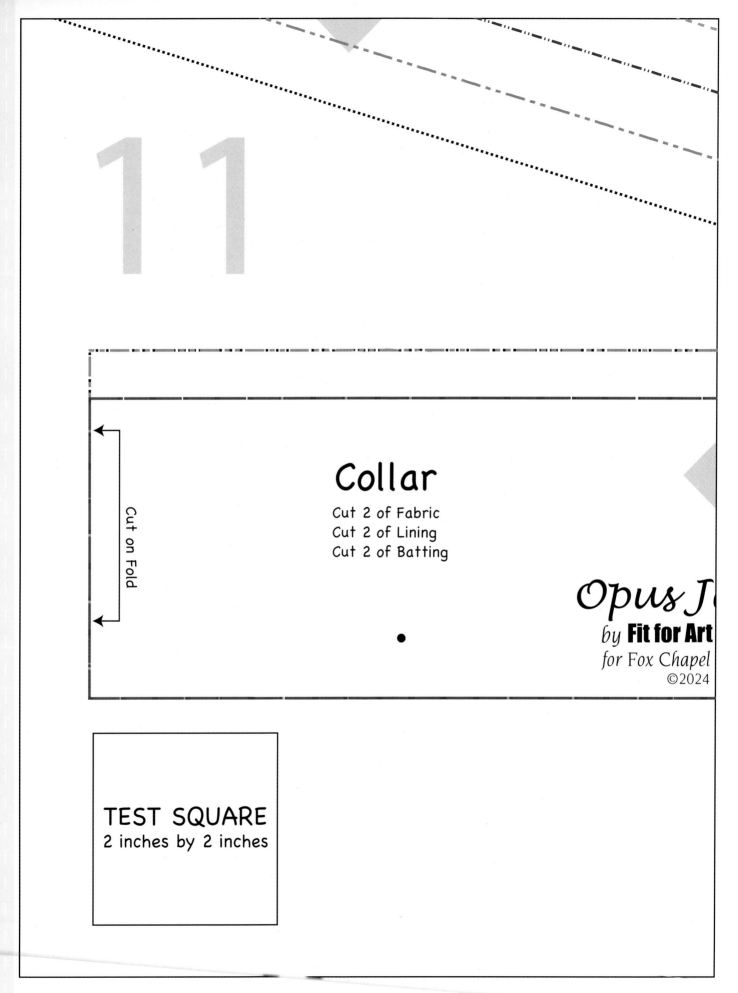

11

Collar

Cut 2 of Fabric
Cut 2 of Lining
Cut 2 of Batting

Cut on Fold

Opus J
by **Fit for Art**
for Fox Chapel
©2024

TEST SQUARE
2 inches by 2 inches

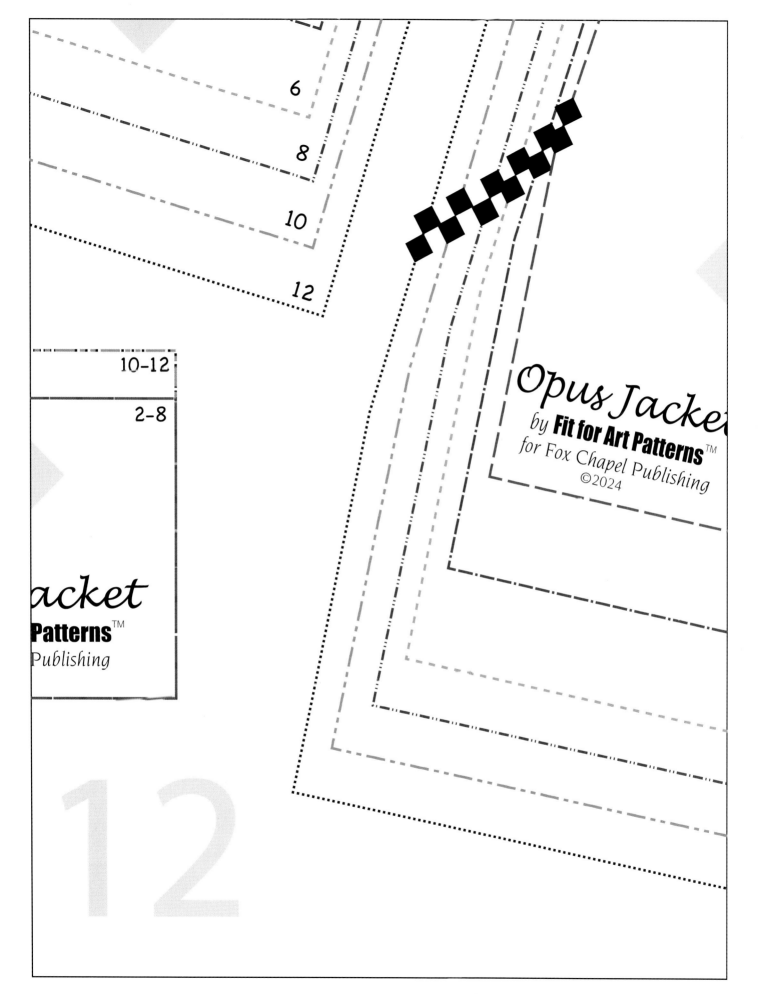

6

8

10

12

10–12

2–8

acket

Patterns™

Publishing

12

Opus Jacket
_by_ **Fit for Art Patterns**™
for Fox Chapel Publishing
©2024

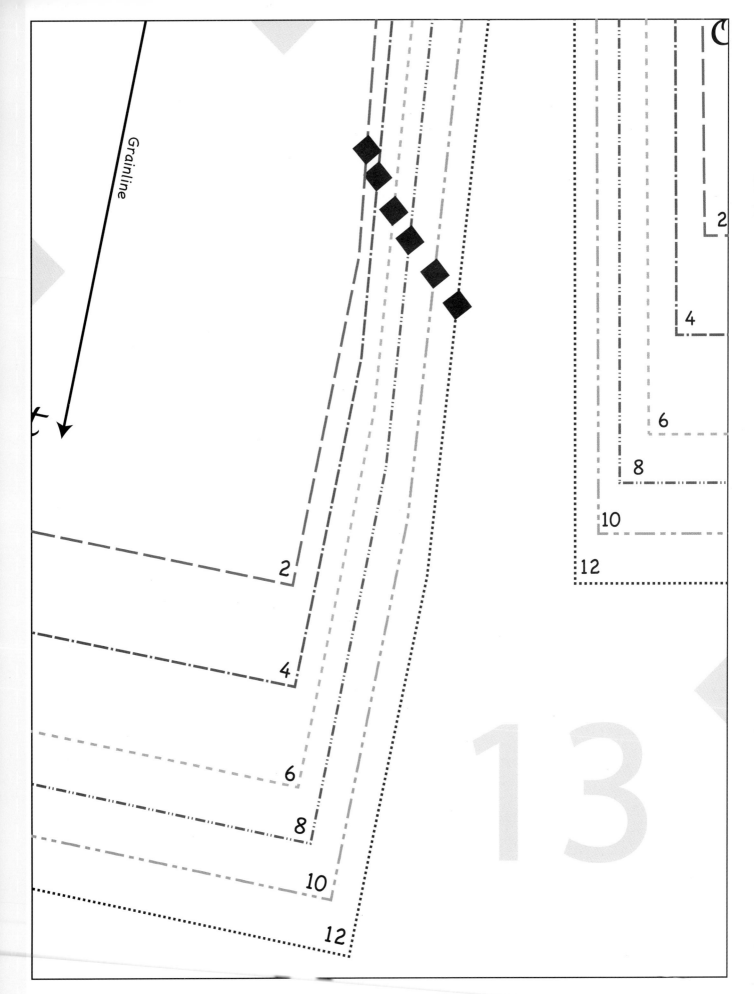

Grainline

2
4
6
8
10
12

2
4
6
8
10
12

13

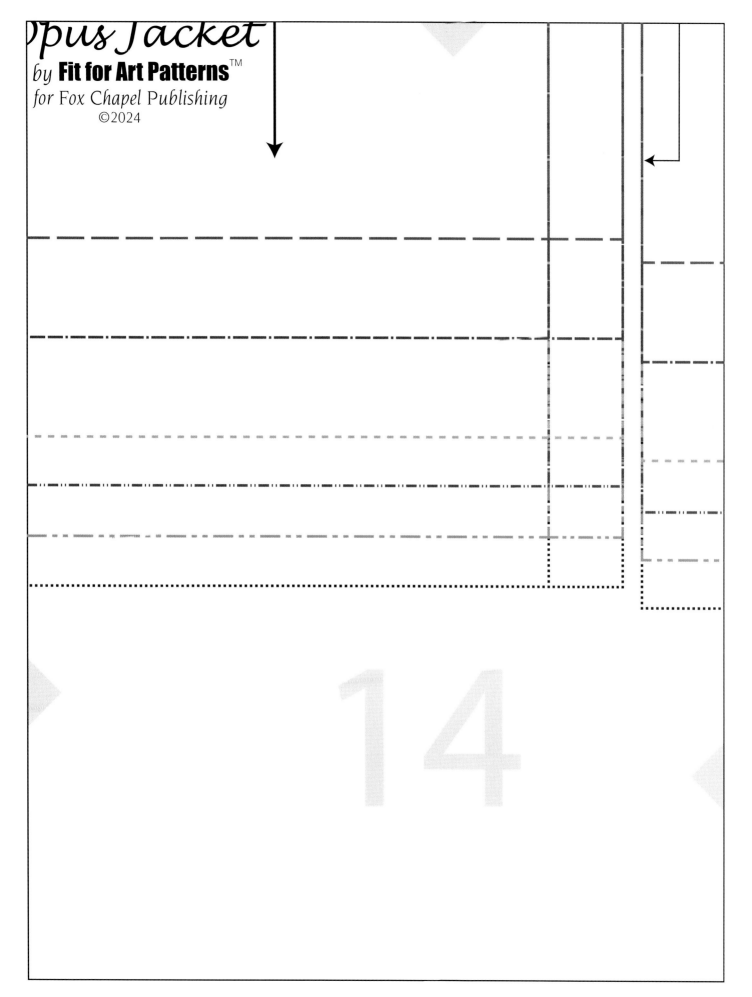

Opus Jacket
by Fit for Art Patterns™
for Fox Chapel Publishing
©2024

14

Opus Jacket

by Fit for Art Patterns™

for Fox Chapel Publishing
©2024

2

4

6

8

10

12

15

Index

Index

Conversion Charts

Inches	Centimeters
⅛"	0.3cm
¼"	0.6cm
⅜"	1cm
½"	1.3cm
⅝"	1.6cm
¾"	1.9cm
1"	2.5cm
1¼"	3.2cm
1½"	3.8cm
2"	5.1cm
2¼"	5.7cm
2⅜"	6cm
2¾"	7cm
3"	7.6cm
3½"	8.9cm
3¾"	9.5cm
4"	10.2cm
4¼"	10.8cm
4½"	11.4cm
5"	12.7cm
6"	15.2cm
6½"	16.5cm
7"	17.8cm
7¼"	18.4cm
8"	20.3cm
8½"	21.6cm
9"	22.9cm
10"	25.4cm
11"	27.9cm
21"	53.3cm
22"	55.9cm
23"	58.4cm
24"	61cm
25"	63.5cm
25½"	64.8cm
26"	66cm
27"	68.6cm
27½"	69.9cm
28"	71.2cm
28½"	72.4cm
29"	73.7cm
30"	76.2cm
31"	78.7cm
32"	81.3cm
33"	83.8cm
33½"	85.1cm
34"	86.4cm
36"	91.4cm
36½"	92.7cm

Inches	Centimeters
37"	94cm
38"	96.5cm
39"	99.1cm
40"	101.6cm
40½"	102.9cm
41"	104.1cm
42"	106.7cm
43"	109.2cm
44"	111.8cm
45"	114.3cm
46"	116.8cm
47"	119.4cm
49"	124.5cm
50"	127cm
51"	129.5cm
52"	132.1cm
53"	134.6cm
54"	137.2cm
55"	139.7cm
57"	144.8cm
58"	147.3cm
61"	154.9cm
62"	157.5cm
63"	160cm
65"	165.1cm
72"	182.9cm
100"	254cm
135"	342.9cm
160"	406.4cm

Yards	Meters
¼ yard	0.2m
½ yard	0.5m
1 yard	0.9m
1¼ yards	1.1m
1½ yards	1.4m
1¾ yards	1.6m
2 yards	1.8m
2½ yards	2.3m
2¾ yards	2.5m
3 yards	2.7m
3¾ yards	3.4m
4½ yards	4.1m

Acknowledgments

The sewing world is full of creative and generous people who have helped us compile the projects and designs for this book and inspired us along the way. At the risk of missing a few, we'd like to express our gratitude to the following individuals and businesses that have supported this project as well as those who have encouraged our work over many years.

Thanks to the creative editors and marketing team at Fox Chapel Publishing, who guided us on this journey, and especially Amelia who embraced our concept at the very beginning and advocated for the book. Our thanks to Alison at Alison Cooper Design and Madeline at Goheen Designs, who provided invaluable assistance with graphic design and the digital patterns for the Opus Jacket. Design ideas and support for the project were provided by Diane and Bruce at SewBatik, Judy and her team at Artistic Artifacts, Kat at Capital Quilts, Michelle at Dusty's Vintage Buttons, Aline at Antique Textile Shop, Amanda at Winners Circle Marketing, Christine at Armstrong Studio, Carol at *Threads* magazine, and the team at *Classic Sewing* magazine. In addition, we'd like to extend a special thanks to Laura Murray and Floris Flam, who taught us so many of the tricks that make sewing quilted jackets easier. Throughout our sewing business journey, we've been supported by our professional colleagues and friends in the Association of Sewing and Design Professionals, including Edye Sanford, Susan Khalje, and Sarah Veblen.

Materials for the projects in this book were provided by: Hobbs Batting, Quilters Dream Batting, Riley Blake Fabrics, SewBatik Fabrics, Sulky, Aurifil, Oliso, and Fit for Art's stash.

Last but by no means least, we tip our hats to our husbands, Jim and Darrell, who have believed in our dreams, given us the time and space to accomplish them, and cooked for us when the deadlines were intense. This book is a celebration of friendship and creative collaboration that evolved into Fit for Art Patterns 14 years ago after nearly 25 years of sewing together for fun.

About the Authors

Rae Cumbie has woven her creative magic into the fabric of the fashion industry for more than three decades. Rae began by crafting custom clothing for women and children in her home-based studio. Soon, she became one of Baltimore's most sought-after dressmakers, earning the title of "Baltimore's Best Tailor" from *Baltimore* magazine.

Her passion for wearable art and her expertise in jacket construction led Rae to teach jacket making to weavers. She envisioned a pattern that offered the versatility and fit that textile artists wanted. This vision led to a grant from the Potomac Fiber Arts Guild, which ultimately resulted in the Tabula Rasa Jacket pattern.

In 2011, Rae and Carrie Emerson founded Fit for Art Patterns. Rae's role as Creative Director allows her to educate and inspire a community of sewists with her popular weekly blog, "Sew! Let's Get Dressed," and through her contributions to notable publications like *Threads* magazine. Her dedication to the craft has been further evidenced by her leadership roles, including serving as president of the Association of Sewing and Design Professionals.

Rae and her husband, Jim, have two daughters. She divides her time between her studios in Baltimore, Maryland, and Durfort, France.

A nationally respected teacher and author, Rae inspires sewists and the Fit for Art community to learn new skills, express their creativity, and sew themselves the wardrobe of their dreams.

Carrie Emerson, the Managing Director of Fit for Art Patterns, skillfully blends her legal expertise and passion for sewing to run and grow the thriving independent pattern company. Her sewing projects began with a simple quilt in middle school home economics and have evolved through the years into sophisticated garments that integrate piecing, quilting, and elements of her mother's weaving.

Before turning to more creative pursuits, Carrie dedicated a decade to serving as an assistant attorney general in Maryland. Her transition to the arts included 10 years as a docent at the Walters Art Museum, giving tours to school groups. It was during this time that Carrie and Rae, whose husbands both started at the same law firm on the same day, formed a deep bond. This friendship laid the foundation for Fit for Art Patterns, which they launched together in 2011.

At Fit for Art Patterns, Carrie has refined her skills in sewing, pattern drafting, and garment fitting. The meticulous attention to detail and organizational skills she developed during her legal career have proven to be instrumental in managing the business side of the company.

Carrie and her husband, Darrell, live in Baltimore. They have two children.

Carrie's unique ability to manage the company's operations while embracing her creative side has played a crucial role in shaping the success of Fit for Art Patterns.